SCHAUM'S *Easy* OUTLINES

QUANTUM

MECHANICS

D0469607

Other Books in Schaum's Easy Outline Series Include:

SCHAUM'S *Easy* OUTLINES

QUANTUM MECHANICS

BASED ON SCHAUM'S
Outline of Theory and Problems of Quantum Mechanics
BY
YOAV PELEG, Ph.D.
REUVEN PNINI, Ph.D.
ELYAHU ZAARUR, M.Sc.

ABRIDGEMENT EDITOR:
LORETTA JOHNSON, Ph.D.

SCHAUM'S OUTLINE SERIES
McGRAW-HILL

New York   Chicago   San Francisco   Lisbon   London   Madrid   Mexico City
Milan   New Delhi   San Juan   Seoul   Singapore   Sydney   Toronto

YOAV PELEG received his Ph.D. in physics from the Technion Institute of Technology in Haifa, Israel. He has published dozens of articles, mostly in the area of general relativity and quantum cosmology. He is a researcher with Motorola Israel.

REUVEN PNINI received his Ph.D. in physics from the Technion Institute of Technology in Haifa, Israel. He has published several articles, mostly in the area of condensed matter physics. He is the chief scientific editor of Rakefet Publishing, Ltd.

ELYAHU ZAARUR received his master of science in physics from the Technion Institute of Technology in Haifa. He has published more than a dozen books on physics. He is currently the managing director of Rakefet Publishing, Ltd.

LORETTA JOHNSON teaches physics, including courses in quantum mechanics, at Kalamazoo College in Michigan. She previously taught at Grinnell College in Iowa and Drury College in Missouri. She received a B.S. from Grinnell College and both her M.S. and Ph.D. in physics from the University of Kansas. She is interested in neutrino oscillations and interactions and has published several papers on neutrinos.

1 2 3 4 5 6 7 8 9 DOC/DOC 0 9 8 7 6 5

ISBN 0-07-145533-7

Contents

Chapter 1
PHYSICAL
BACKGROUND

In This Chapter:

- ✔ *Introduction*
- ✔ *Light Has Wave and Particle Properties*
- ✔ *Matter Has Particle and Wave Properties*
- ✔ *Uncertainty*
- ✔ *Atoms and Spectra*

Introduction

Out of a diverse and confusing morass of experiments beginning in the nineteenth century, gradually a simple, if bizarre, theory called quantum mechanics emerged in the early twentieth century. As the theory was fleshed out, it motivated more experiments, which directed the development of the theory. The quantum mechanics we study here is a little corner of the larger quantum theory, which encompasses quantum field theory and quantum electrodynamics, and in which theory and experiment agree to an astounding precision.

Unlike other fields of physics, there are no comfortable conceptual analogs to aid us in understanding quantum mechanics. Quantum systems behave unlike anything in our ordinary existence, which is why decades passed between the earliest experimental evidence for quantum behavior and the earliest successful theoretical models. This is also why quantum mechanics texts tend to read like recipe books—there is no motivation for why we calculate quantities the way we do other than that it works; when we carry out quantum calculations as prescribed by Schrödinger, Heisenberg, and others, we obtain answers that agree with measurements.

In later chapters we'll learn what these procedures are, but first we will briefly review some of the experimental evidence underpinning quantum mechanics.

Light Has Wave and Particle Properties

When Young studied the interference of light passing through a pair of slits around 1802, his experiments were interpreted as evidence simply that light was a wave. This conclusion was supported in 1850 by Foucault's observation that light travels slower in water than in air. Further evidence in the next couple of decades included Maxwell showing that light consisted of oscillating electric and magnetic fields. That Michelson and Morley failed to observe either, the medium through which light was then believed to travel, in 1887, only required slight, if ugly, corrections to the theory.

But blackbody radiation and the photoelectric effect were also observed in the 1880s, and they proved impossible to accommodate in the wave theory of light. In 1900, Planck proposed the quantum, a particle-like unit of light containing a specific amount of energy, to explain observed blackbody radiation curves. The quantum was mostly considered a mathematical trick, though it gained a bit of acceptance in 1905 when Einstein was able to use it to explain the photoelectric experiments. More than a decade passed before physicists commonly accepted that quanta reflected the particle nature of light.

We must accept that light sometimes behaves like a wave and other times it behaves like a particle. For example, if we perform Young's double slit experiment, we will observe the pattern predicted by particle theory if we put in a detector to see which slit each quantum goes through, but if we remove this detector, we will observe the pattern predicted by wave theory. So is light a particle or a wave? It depends upon what kind of experiment we perform.

You Need to Know ✔

An essential feature of quantum mechanics is that how we conduct our experiments affects what results we will observe.

Matter Has Particle and Wave Properties

The particle properties of matter have been well known for a long time, but in 1923, a graduate student named de Broglie suggested that since special relativity demonstrated that matter and energy are intimately connected, matter should have wave properties in addition to particle properties, just as light has both wave and particle properties. Using a similar procedure to relate wave and particle properties, he introduced the de Broglie wavelength of matter. This wavelength is generally so tiny that it is unobservable.

However, only a couple years after de Broglie's proposal, Davisson and Germer accidentally discovered that tests of the theory were technologically feasible. Their observation of electron diffraction off large nickel crystals provided the first evidence for the wave nature of particles. More recently, electron interference in a two-slit experiment has been demonstrated, and wave-like behavior has been observed for protons, atoms, and molecules.

Uncertainty

Already we've had to accept that we have no conceptual analogies to help us learn quantum mechanics and that whether light and matter behave as waves or particles depends on what kinds of experiments we're running. For the classically-trained physicist, what's even worse is that we can rarely make definite predictions in quantum mechanics. Unlike classical mechanics where we can use the initial momentum of a baseball to predict precisely where it will land, in quantum mechanics, the best we can do is give the relative likelihood of each of the possible outcomes.

This uncertainty has nothing to do with mistakes or measurement limitations, nor does it arise from failing to study enough. Rather, this uncertainty is an integral feature of quantum mechanics and of nature. A thousand students could each prepare a quantum system so that each system was in exactly the same initial state, and then they could each make exactly the same kind of measurement on the system using the best equipment available, and the result would still be a distribution of different answers. The good news is that the distribution of measured answers would resemble the probability distribution calculated using quantum mechanics, and the average of the students' measurements would be very close to the expectation value predicted by quantum mechanics.

Some aspects of quantum uncertainty have been quantified by Heisenberg's uncertainty principle, which says that we can't know precisely the position and momentum of a particle at the same time. Groping for an explanation for this weird idea that our still-too-classical minds could grasp, physicists have long and often suggested that the uncertainty principle only means that in order to determine the position of a quantum particle very precisely, we must probe it with something that imparts such a big momentum kick to it that it destroys any information about what the momentum was before we looked. But experiments in the past several years have proven that the uncertainty principle holds even when we find sneaky ways to avoid imparting big momentum kicks.

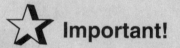 **Important!**

In quantum mechanics, we calculate probabilities and averages because of the uncertainty inherent in quantum systems.

Atoms and Spectra

In 1814, Fraunhofer noticed that the sun's spectrum was not continuous but contained some black lines. Later these were recognized as absorption lines corresponding to the elements in the outer atmosphere of the sun. Measurements of the emission lines of hydrogen and helium in the mid to late nineteenth century allowed Balmer, Rydberg, and others to develop phenomenological models for the emission lines in the 1880s; that is, they didn't understand why the equations should look the way they did, but the equations gave answers that agreed with experiments. Then, in 1896, Zeeman observed that the spectral lines split into several distinct lines if the source of the light was placed in a magnetic field.

It wasn't until 1913 that Bohr finally developed his famous semiclassical atomic model that can fairly well predict the spectral lines of hydrogen. In the Bohr model, electrons are constrained to circular orbits of specific energy and angular momentum. Discrete spectral lines are observed because in order for an electron to move from one orbit to another, it must either absorb or emit exactly the right amount of energy to jump. The quantum mechanical atom we'll study later does away with circular orbits, but it maintains specific energy levels and angular momenta, and its predictions are in good agreement with experiments.

Another decade passed before the magnetic splitting observed by Zeeman could be fairly well explained. This required recognition that electrons have both orbital and intrinsic angular momenta, and each of these contributes a magnetic moment that can be affected by external magnetic fields. This can change slightly the energy levels within atoms, and that also changes the energy difference for an electron to jump, changing the color of light emitted.

Remember

The energy of a photon of light emitted by an atom is equal to the initial energy of the electron in the new energy level it falls to.

Chapter 2
MATHEMATICAL
BACKGROUND

Vector Spaces Over the Complex Field

Wave functions, ψ, in quantum mechanics are complex functions that can be represented as vectors, $|\psi\rangle$, in Hilbert space. Hilbert space is a vector space that is complete and in which there is a scalar (inner) product and a norm related to the scalar product. We represent the scalar product of vectors u and v as $\langle u | v \rangle$.

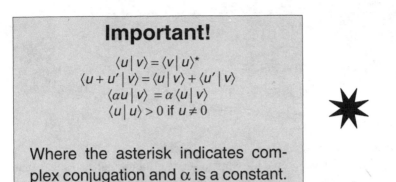

Important!

$$\langle u \mid v \rangle = \langle v \mid u \rangle^*$$
$$\langle u + u' \mid v \rangle = \langle u \mid v \rangle + \langle u' \mid v \rangle$$
$$\langle \alpha u \mid v \rangle = \alpha \langle u \mid v \rangle$$
$$\langle u \mid u \rangle > 0 \text{ if } u \neq 0$$

Where the asterisk indicates complex conjugation and α is a constant.

Just as $\hat{i}, \hat{j}, \hat{k}$ are crucial in Cartesian three-space, we will need an orthonormal basis in Hilbert space. The norm of a vector in our notation is $\|v\| = \sqrt{\langle v \mid v \rangle}$, and if this quantity is one, then we call $\mid v \rangle$ a unit vector and say it is *normalized*. *Orthogonal* vectors satisfy $\langle u \mid v \rangle = 0$. A set of vectors $\{u_i\}$ is *orthonormal* if

$$\langle u_i \mid u_j \rangle = \delta_{ij}$$

for all i and j where δ_{ij} is the *Kronecker delta function*, which is zero for $i \neq j$ and one otherwise.

Solved Problem 2.1 Show that zz^* and $z + z^*$ are real if $z = a + bi$ where a and b are real.

Solution. $zz^* = (a + bi)(a - bi) = a^2 + b^2 = |z|^2$
$ z + z^* = (a + bi) + (a - bi) = 2a$

Operators, Eigenvectors, and Eigenvalues

State vectors in quantum mechanics can be represented as column vectors, and operators as matrices. A linear operator, T, may act on a state such that $\langle Tu \mid v \rangle = \langle u \mid T^\dagger v \rangle$, where $T^\dagger$ is the *hermitian conjugate* of T, found by taking the complex conjugate of the transpose of T. There are several important classes of operators that are distinguished by the relationship of T and $T^\dagger$.

Remember

$T = T^\dagger$ for hermitian T
$T = -T^\dagger$ for anti-hermitian T
$\langle Tu \mid Tv \rangle = \langle u \mid v \rangle$ for unitary T
$TT^\dagger = T^\dagger T$ for normal T

We will need to find a complete set of orthonormal states that span the Hilbert space. The set that is most easily obtained is the set of *stationary states* (not time-dependent) that satisfy an equation of the form $T \mid v \rangle = \lambda \mid v \rangle$. The states that satisfy this *eigenvalue equation* are called *eigenvectors*, and the λ are the corresponding *eigenvalues*. When these are expressed as matrices, the usual methods of linear algebra can be employed.

Solved Problem 2.2 Show that the eigenvalues of an hermitian operator are real.

Solution. Suppose that λ is an eigenvalue of T and $T = T^\dagger$. For every $v \neq 0$ in the Hilbert space,

$$\lambda \langle v \mid v \rangle = \langle \lambda v \mid v \rangle = \langle Tv \mid v \rangle = \langle v \mid Tv \rangle = \langle v \mid \lambda v \rangle = \langle \lambda v \mid v \rangle^* = \lambda^* \langle v \mid v \rangle$$

Since $\langle v \mid v \rangle$ is a real positive number, it follows that $\lambda = \lambda^*$, so λ is a real number.

 **Note!**

The fact that the eigenvalues of hermitian operators are real is of great importance since these eigenvalues represent measurable quantities.

Fourier Series and the Fourier Transform

Consider a function $f(x)$ over the interval $0 < x < \ell$ that is in the set of all square integrable functions. These functions exist in an infinite dimensional vector space denoted $L_2 \, (0, \ell)$ for which the inner product is

$$\langle f | g \rangle = \int_0^\ell f(x) g(x) * dx$$

Every function $L_2 \, (0, \ell)$ in can be expanded in a Fourier series,

$$f(x) = \sum_{n=-\infty}^{\infty} f_n e^{i k_n x} \quad \text{where} \quad k_n = \frac{2\pi}{\ell} n$$

We can consider these exponential functions as a basis of the infinite dimensional space. The coefficients f_n in the expansion are called Fourier coefficients and are determined using the relation

$$f_n = \frac{1}{\ell} \int_0^\ell f(t) e^{-i k_n t} dt$$

Now consider a function $f(x)$ defined on $(-\infty, \infty)$ that is not necessarily periodic. The numbers k_n become progressively denser until we have in the limit a continuous range of functions, e^{ikx}. This is the intuitive basis of the following result:

$$f(x) = \frac{1}{\sqrt{2\pi}} \int_{-\infty}^{\infty} F(k) e^{ikx} dx$$

where

$$F(k) = \frac{1}{\sqrt{2\pi}} \int_{-\infty}^{\infty} f(x) e^{-ikx} dx$$

$F(k)$ and $f(x)$ are said to be *Fourier transforms* of each other.
Fourier transforms will prove particularly useful since configuration space (x, y, z) and momentum space (P_x, P_y, P_z) are related in this way.

The Dirac Delta Function

Previously we used the Kronecker delta function, δ_{mn}, which returns the value one whenever the integers n and m are equal and zero otherwise. There is a continuous analogue, the Dirac delta function defined by

$$\delta(x) = \infty \text{ for } x = 0 \text{ and } 0 \text{ otherwise}$$

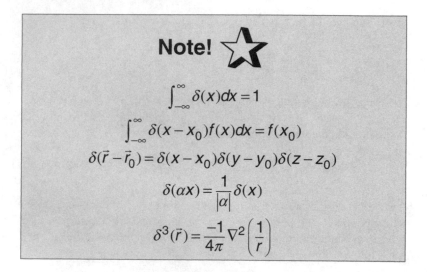

Note!

$$\int_{-\infty}^{\infty} \delta(x)dx = 1$$

$$\int_{-\infty}^{\infty} \delta(x - x_0)f(x)dx = f(x_0)$$

$$\delta(\vec{r} - \vec{r}_0) = \delta(x - x_0)\delta(y - y_0)\delta(z - z_0)$$

$$\delta(\alpha x) = \frac{1}{|\alpha|}\delta(x)$$

$$\delta^3(\vec{r}) = \frac{-1}{4\pi}\nabla^2\left(\frac{1}{r}\right)$$

Although we call this the Dirac delta function, it is in fact a distribution or functional.

Solved Problem 2.3 Evaluate the following integrals:

(a) $\displaystyle\int_{-\infty}^{\infty} (ax + b)\delta(x)dx,$

(b) $\displaystyle\int_{0}^{\infty} \left(\cos^2 x + 4x + 4\right)\delta(x + 3)dx,$

(c) $\displaystyle\int_{-1}^{1} \left(12x^2 + 5x + 3\right)\delta\left(x - \frac{1}{2}\right)dx.$

Solution.

(a) The delta function is at $x = 0$ which is clearly within the limits of integration, so we just evaluate the function at that point.

$$\int_{-\infty}^{\infty} (ax + b)\delta(x)\,dx = b$$

(b) The delta function is at $x = -3$ which is not within the range of integration, so it will integrate to zero.

$$\int_{0}^{\infty} \left(\cos^2 x + 4x + 4\right)\delta(x+3)\,dx = 0$$

(c) The delta function is at $x = \dfrac{1}{2}$ which is within the limits of integration so we just evaluate the function at that point.

$$\int_{-1}^{1} \left(12x^2 + 5x + 3\right)\delta\left(x - \frac{1}{2}\right)dx = 12\left(\frac{1}{2}\right)^2 + 5\left(\frac{1}{2}\right) + 3 = \frac{17}{2}$$

Chapter 3
THE SCHRÖDINGER EQUATION

IN THIS CHAPTER:

✔ *Wave Function of a Single Particle*
✔ *The Schrödinger Equation*
✔ *Particle in a Time-Independent Potential*
✔ *Operators*

Wave Function of a Single Particle

In quantum mechanics, a particle is characterized by a *wave function*, $\Psi(\vec{r},t)$, which contains information about the spatial state of the particle at time t. The wave function is a complex function of three coordinates, x, y, z and of time, and it must be defined and continuous everywhere. The interpretation of the wave function is that the probability, $dP(\vec{r},t)$, of the particle being in a volume element $d^3r = dxdydz$ located at the point $\vec{r}$ is

$$dP(\vec{r},t) = C|\Psi(\vec{r},t)|^2 \, d^3r$$

Where C is a normalization constant. The *total probability* of finding the particle anywhere in space at time t is equal to unity, $\int dP(\vec{r},t) = 1$. To satisfy these relationships, the wave function must be square-integrable so the integral is finite and the normalization constant is given by

$$\frac{1}{C} = \int \left| \Psi\left(\vec{r},t\right) \right|^2 d^3r$$

When $C = 1$ we say that the wave function is *normalized*.

Consider a particle described by a normalized wave function. The *probability density* is defined by

$$\rho\left(\vec{r},t\right) = \left| \Psi\left(\vec{r},t\right) \right|^2$$

The integral of $\rho(\vec{r},t)$ over all space remains constant at all times. Note that this does not mean that $\rho(\vec{r},t)$ must be time independent at every point in space. Nevertheless, we can express a local *conservation of probability* in the form of a *continuity equation*

$$\frac{\partial \rho\left(\vec{r},t\right)}{\partial t} + \vec{\nabla} \cdot J\left(\vec{r},t\right) = 0$$

where J is the *probability current*, defined by

$$\vec{J}\left(\vec{r},t\right) = \frac{\hbar}{2mi}\left[\Psi^*\left(\vec{\nabla}\Psi\right) - \Psi\left(\vec{\nabla}\Psi^*\right) \right]$$

We can define reflection and transmission coefficients using the probability current by considering a particle (or stream of particles) moving from one region of constant potential, V_1, to a second region with some other constant potential, V_2, possibly passing over or through a potential step or barrier. In region one, the state is composed of the incoming wave with probability current J_I and a reflected wave of probability current J_R. In region two, there is a transmitted wave of probability current J_T. The *reflection* and *transmission coefficients* are defined by

$$R \equiv \left| \frac{J_R}{J_I} \right|$$

$$T = \left| \frac{J_T}{J_I} \right|$$

respectively.

Solved Problem 3.1 Consider the wave function

$$\Psi(x,t) = \left[Ae^{ipx/\hbar} + Be^{-ipx/\hbar} \right] e^{-ip^2 t/2m\hbar}$$

Find the probability current corresponding to this wave function.

Solution. Taking the complex conjugate of this, using the definitions,

$$A^* A = |A|^2$$

$$\left(e^{ipx/\hbar} \right)^* = e^{-ipx/\hbar}$$

$$\left(e^{-ip^2 t/2m\hbar} \right)^* e^{-ip^2 t/2m\hbar} = 1$$

and plugging into the definition of probability current yields

$$J = \frac{p}{m} \left[|A|^2 - |B|^2 \right]$$

Notice that the wave function expresses a superposition of two currents of particles moving in opposite directions. The current of amplitude $|A|^2$ moves to the right with momentum p, and the current of amplitude $|B|^2$ moves to the left with the same magnitude of momentum.

The Schrödinger Equation

Consider a particle of mass m subjected to a potential $V(\vec{r},t)$. The time evolution of the wave function is governed by the *Schrödinger equation*.

You Need to Know ✔

The Schrödinger equation is

$$\frac{-\hbar^2}{2m}\nabla^2\Psi(\vec{r},t)+V(\vec{r},t)\Psi(\vec{r},t)=i\hbar\frac{\partial\Psi(\vec{r},t)}{\partial t}$$

where ∇^2 is the *Laplacian operator*

$$\nabla^2=\frac{\partial^2}{\partial x^2}+\frac{\partial^2}{\partial y^2}+\frac{\partial^2}{\partial z^2}$$

The Schrödinger equation is a linear, homogeneous differential equation in Ψ. Consequently, the *superposition principle* holds; that is, if $\Psi_1, \Psi_2,$ $\cdots, \Psi_n$ are solutions of the Schrödinger equation, then

$$\Psi=\sum_{i=1}^{n}\alpha_i\Psi_i(\vec{r},t)$$

is also a solution. Notice that the Schrödinger equation is first order in time, so the state at an initial time determines the wave function at later times.

Solved Problem 3.2 Consider a particle subjected to a time-independent potential, $V(\vec{r})$.

(a) Assume that a state of the particle is described by a wave function of the form $\Psi(\vec{r},t) = \psi(\vec{r})\phi(t)$, and show that $\phi(t) = Ae^{-iEt/\hbar}$ and that $\psi(\vec{r})$ must satisfy the equation

$$\frac{-\hbar^2}{2m}\nabla^2\psi(\vec{r})+V(\vec{r})\psi(\vec{r})=E\psi(\vec{r})$$

where A and E are constants and where m is the mass of the particle.

(b) Prove that these solutions of the Schrödinger equation lead to a time-independent probability density.

Solution.

(a) Substituting in we find

$$\varphi(t)\left[\frac{-\hbar^2}{2m}\nabla^2\psi(\vec{r})\right]+\varphi(t)V(\vec{r})\psi(\vec{r})=i\hbar\psi(\vec{r})\frac{d\varphi(t)}{dt}$$

We could now accomplish *separation of variables* by dividing by $\phi(t)$ to get all the time dependence out of the left-hand side and dividing by $\psi(\vec{r})$ to get all the space dependence out of the right-hand side:

$$\frac{1}{\psi(\vec{r})}\left[\frac{-\hbar^2}{2m}\nabla^2\psi(\vec{r})\right]+V(\vec{r})=\frac{i\hbar}{\varphi(t)}\frac{d\varphi(t)}{dt}$$

Since all the position dependence is on one side of the equation and all the time dependence is on the other side, each side must independently be equal to the same constant, which we will call E. We can immediately recognize a familiar differential equation for time

$$\frac{d\varphi(t)}{dt}=\frac{E}{i\hbar}\varphi(t)$$

and recall that the solution is simply an exponential:

$$\varphi(t)=Ae^{-iEt/\hbar}$$

The equation for the spatial dependence is

$$\frac{-\hbar^2}{2m}\nabla^2\psi(\vec{r})+V(\vec{r})\psi(\vec{r})=E\psi(\vec{r})$$

(b) Since we don't know the form of ψ, we might as well absorb the constant from the time dependence into it, allowing us to express the full wave function as $\Psi(\vec{r},t)=\psi(\vec{r})e^{i\omega t}$, so the probability density is

$$\rho\left(\vec{r},t\right)=\left|\Psi\right|^2=\left[\psi\left(\vec{r}\right)e^{-i\omega t}\right]^*\left[\psi\left(\vec{r}\right)e^{-i\omega t}\right]=\left|\psi\left(\vec{r}\right)\right|^2 e^{i\omega t}e^{-i\omega t}=\left|\psi\left(\vec{r}\right)\right|^2$$

The lack of any time dependence in the probability density is why this type of solution is called *stationary*.

Particle in a Time-Independent Potential

The wave function of a particle subjected to a time-independent potential, $V(\vec{r})$, satisfies the time-independent Schrödinger equation.

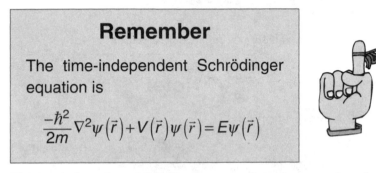

Remember

The time-independent Schrödinger equation is

$$\frac{-\hbar^2}{2m}\nabla^2\psi\left(\vec{r}\right)+V\left(\vec{r}\right)\psi\left(\vec{r}\right)=E\psi\left(\vec{r}\right)$$

The time independence of V allows us to perform the separation of variables, $\Psi(\vec{r},t)=\psi(\vec{r})\phi(t)$, as we showed in the earlier problem.

Suppose that at time $t=0$ we have $\Psi(\vec{r}, 0) = \sum_{n} \psi_n(\vec{r})$ where $\psi_n(\vec{r})$ are the spatial parts of stationary states,

$$\Psi_n\left(\vec{r},t\right)=\psi\left(\vec{r}\right)e^{-i\omega_n t}$$

where $E_n = \hbar\omega_n$. In this case, according to the superposition principle, the time evolution is described by

$$\Psi\left(\vec{r},t\right)=\sum_{n}\psi_n\left(\vec{r}\right)e^{-i\omega_n t}$$

Thus if we know the initial wave function, we need only express it in terms of the stationary states in order to determine the wave function at all future times.

For a *free particle*, we have $V(\vec{r},t)=0$, and the Schrödinger equation is satisfied by solutions of the form

$$\Psi(\vec{r},t) = Ae^{i(\vec{k}\cdot\vec{r}-\omega t)}$$

where A is a constant and k satisfies the relationship $2m\omega = \hbar k^2$. Solutions of this form are called *plane waves*. Note that since in this case the Ψ are not square integrable, they *cannot rigorously* represent a particle. On the other hand, a superposition of plane waves *can* yield an expression that is square integrable and can therefore describe the dynamics of a particle:

$$\Psi(\vec{r},t) = \frac{1}{(2\pi)^{3/2}} \int g(\vec{k}) e^{i\left[\vec{k}\cdot\vec{r}-\omega(\vec{k})t\right]} d^3k$$

A wave function of this form is called a *wave packet*.

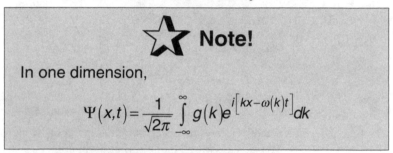

☆ **Note!**

In one dimension,

$$\Psi(x,t) = \frac{1}{\sqrt{2\pi}} \int_{-\infty}^{\infty} g(k) e^{i\left[kx-\omega(k)t\right]} dk$$

Solved Problem 3.3 Consider a particle of mass m held in a one-dimensional potential $V(x)$. Suppose that in some region the potential is constant, $V(x) = V_0$. For this region, find the stationary states of the particle when (a) $E > V_0$, (b) $E < V_0$, and (c) $E = V_0$, where E is the energy of the particle.

Solution.

(a) Rearranging the Schrödinger equation we find

$$\frac{d^2\psi(x)}{dx^2} = \frac{2m}{-\hbar^2}\left[E-V_0\right]\psi(x)$$

and recognize the familiar differential equation where the second derivative of the function gives the same function times a constant. For $E > V_0$, the constant is negative and the solutions are sines and cosines or complex exponentials. It is convenient to introduce the positive constant k such that $k^2 = 2m(E - V_0)/\hbar^2$ so that the solution can be written

$$\psi(x) = Ae^{ikx} + A'e^{-ikx}$$

where A, A' are complex coefficients to be determined by boundary conditions.

(b) For $E < V_0$, it is convenient to introduce the positive constant η such that $\eta^2 = 2m(V_0 - E)/\hbar^2$. This simplifies a familiar differential equation whose solutions are real exponentials:

$$\psi(x) = Be^{\eta x} + B'e^{-\eta x}$$

where B, B' are complex coefficients to be determined by boundary conditions.

(c) When $E = V_0$, we have $\dfrac{d^2\psi(x)}{dx^2} = 0$, so $\psi(x)$ has no curvature and is thus a linear function,

$$\psi(x) = Cx + C'$$

where C, C' are complex coefficients to be determined by boundary conditions.

Solved Problem 3.4 Consider a particle of mass m confined in an infinite one-dimensional potential well of width a:

$$V(x) = 0 \text{ if } \frac{-a}{2} \le x \le \frac{a}{2}$$

$$V(x) = \infty \text{ otherwise}$$

Find the energy eigenstates of the Hamiltonian (i.e. the stationary states) and the corresponding eigenenergies.

Solution. Outside the well the potential is infinite, so there's no chance of finding the particle there,

$$\psi(x) = 0 \text{ for } |x| > \frac{a}{2}$$

This imposes the *boundary conditions* at $\pm a/2$ that the wave function must be zero there. We may now exploit the results of the previous problem to determine the possible eigenstates and eigenenergies.

$E > 0$: The wave function at each boundary being zero gives

$$Ae^{-ika/2} + A'e^{ika/2} = 0$$

$$Ae^{ika/2} + A'e^{-ika/2} = 0$$

The first gives $A = -A'e^{ika}$. Substituting this into the second gives

$$A'\left[-e^{3ika/2} + e^{-ika/2}\right] = 0$$

If the overall coefficient is zero, then we have the trivial case of no solution ($\Psi = 0$); therefore, the term inside the brackets must be zero, and we are free to multiply it by anything, for example, $e^{-ika/2}$. This will yield $e^{-ika} - e^{ika} = -2i\sin(ka) = 0$ which is only true when $ka = n\pi$, where n is a positive integer. From the definition of k, we arrive at the eigenenergies:

$$E_n = \frac{\hbar^2 k_n^2}{2m} = \frac{\hbar^2}{2m}\left(\frac{n\pi}{a}\right)^2 = \frac{(n\pi\hbar)^2}{2ma^2}$$

The corresponding eigenfunctions are

$$\psi_n(x) = C\sin\left[n\pi\left(\frac{x}{a} - \frac{1}{2}\right)\right]$$

The normalization constant is determined from

$$\frac{1}{C^2} = \int_{-a/2}^{a/2} \sin^2\left[n\pi\left(\frac{x}{a} - \frac{1}{2}\right)\right] dx = \frac{a}{2}$$

so that

$$\psi_n(x) = \sqrt{\frac{2}{a}}\sin\left[n\pi\left(\frac{x}{a} - \frac{1}{2}\right)\right]$$

_E < 0_: Here the boundary conditions give

$$Be^{-\eta a/2} + B'e^{\eta a/2} = 0$$
$$Be^{\eta a/2} + B'e^{-\eta a/2} = 0$$

Following the same procedure as before, we find these equations lead to the conclusion that $\eta = 0$, which is inconsistent with the assumption that η must be positive. Therefore, there are no solutions with $E < 0$.
_E = 0_: This time the boundary conditions indicate that C, $C' = 0$, so there are no solutions with $E = 0$.

All of the above implies that the lowest energy level in the _infinite square well_ is

$$E_1 = \frac{(\pi\hbar)^2}{2ma^2}$$

Solved Problem 3.5 Consider the step potential:

$$V(x) = V_0 \text{ if } x > 0$$
$$V(x) = 0 \text{ if } x < 0$$

Consider a current of particles of energy $E > V_0$ moving from $x = -\infty$ to the right.

(a) Write the stationary solutions for each of the regions.

(b) Express the fact that there is no current coming back from $x = +\infty$ to the left.

(c) Use the boundary conditions to express the reflected and transmitted amplitudes in terms of the incident amplitude. Note that since the wave function is bounded, it is possible to show that the derivative of the wave function is continuous for all x.

(d) Compute the probability current in each region and interpret each term.

(e) Find the reflection and transmission coefficients.

Solution.

(a) Let region one be on the left and region two on the right, and borrow the results of Solved Problem 3.3a to define

$$k_1 = \sqrt{\frac{2mE}{\hbar^2}}$$

$$k_2 = \sqrt{\frac{2m(E - V_0)}{\hbar^2}}$$

which lead to the solutions

$$\psi_1(x) = A_1 e^{ik_1 x} + A_1' e^{-ik_1 x}$$

$$\psi_2(x) = A_2 e^{ik_2 x} + A_2' e^{-ik_2 x}$$

(b) Since there is nothing moving left in region two, the coefficient for the term representing a wave moving left in region two must be zero, $A_2' = 0$.

(c) Both the wave function and its derivative should be continuous at the boundary:

$$A_1 + A_1' = A_2$$

$$ik_1 A_1 e^{ik_1 x} - ik_1 A_1' e^{-ik_1 x} \,|_{x=0} = ik_2 A_2 e^{ik_2 x} \,|_{x=0}$$

Simplifying and combining we obtain

$$k_1 \left(A_1 - A_1'\right) = k_2 A_2 = k_2 \left(A_1 + A_1'\right)$$

which yields

$$\frac{A_1'}{A_1} = \frac{k_1 - k_2}{k_1 + k_2}$$

and eventually

$$\frac{A_2}{A_1} = \frac{2k_1}{k_1 + k_2}$$

(d) $J_1(x) = \frac{\hbar k_1}{m}\left(|A_1|^2 - |A_1'|^2\right)$ contains both a leftward current and a

reflected current. $J_2(x) = \frac{\hbar k_2}{m}|A_2|^2$ represents only the transmitted current.

(e) The reflection coefficient is

$$R = \frac{|A_1'|^2 \, \hbar k_1/m}{|A_1|^2 \, \hbar k_1/m} = \left|\frac{A_1'}{A_1}\right|^2 = \frac{(k_1 - k_2)^2}{(k_1 + k_2)^2} = 1 - \frac{4k_1k_2}{(k_1 + k_2)^2}$$

which clearly has a value between zero and one. The transmission coefficient is

$$T = \frac{|A_2|^2 \, \hbar k_2/m}{|A_1|^2 \, \hbar k_1/m} = \frac{k_2}{k_1}\left|\frac{A_1'}{A_1}\right|^2 = \frac{(2k_1)^2}{(k_1 + k_2)^2} = \frac{4k_1k_2}{(k_1 + k_2)^2}$$

so that obviously $R + T = 1$.

Solved Problem 3.6 Consider a particle of mass m and energy $E > 0$ held in a one-dimensional potential $-V_0\delta(x - a)$.

(a) Integrate the stationary Schrödinger equation between $a - \varepsilon$ and $a + \varepsilon$. Taking the limit $\varepsilon \to 0$, show that the derivative of the eigenfunction presents a discontinuity at $x = a$ and determine it.

(b) Relying on our previous work, we have $k = \sqrt{2mE/\hbar^2}$ and

$$\psi_1(x) = A_1 e^{ikx} + A_1' e^{-ikx}$$
$$\psi_2(x) = A_2 e^{ikx} + A_2' e^{-ikx}$$

for regions 1 and 2, respectively. Calculate the matrix M defined by

$$\begin{pmatrix} A_2 \\ A_2' \end{pmatrix} = M \begin{pmatrix} A_1 \\ A_1' \end{pmatrix}$$

Solution.

(a) Integrating yields

$$\frac{-\hbar^2}{2m} \int_{a-\varepsilon}^{a+\varepsilon} \frac{d^2\psi(x)}{dx^2} dx + V_0 \int_{a-\varepsilon}^{a+\varepsilon} \delta(x-a)\psi(x) dx = E \int_{a-\varepsilon}^{a+\varepsilon} \psi(x) dx$$

Exploiting the continuity of the wave function and the definition of the delta function, we find that

$$\frac{-\hbar^2}{2m} \left[\frac{d\psi(x)}{dx} \Big|_{x=a-\varepsilon} - \frac{d\psi(x)}{dx} \Big|_{x=a+\varepsilon} \right] + V_0\psi(a) = 0$$

So, the derivative of $\psi(x)$ presents a discontinuity at $x = a$ equal to $2mV_0\psi(a)/\hbar^2$. Any time there's an infinite discontinuity in the potential, there will be a discontinuity in the derivative of the wave function.

(b) The boundary condition from the continuity of $\psi(x)$ at $x = a$ is

$$A_1 e^{ika} + A_1' e^{-ika} = A_2 e^{ika} + A_2' e^{-ika}$$

The discontinuity in the derivative leads to

$$\frac{\hbar^2}{2m} ik \left[A_1 e^{ika} - A_1' e^{-ika} - A_2 e^{ika} + A_2' e^{-ika} \right] = -V_0 \left(A_1 e^{ika} + A_1' e^{-ika} \right)$$

These two equations allow us to express A_2 and A_2' in terms of A_1 and A_1':

$$A_2 = \left(1 + \frac{mV_0}{ik\hbar^2} \right) A_1 + \frac{mV_0}{ik\hbar^2} e^{-2ika} A_1'$$

$$A_2' = -\frac{mV_0}{ik\hbar^2} e^{2ika} A_1 + \left(1 - \frac{mV_0}{ik\hbar^2} \right) A_1'$$

Transferring these results into the matrix gives

$$M = \begin{pmatrix} 1 + \dfrac{mV_0}{ik\hbar^2} & \dfrac{mV_0}{ik\hbar^2} e^{-2ika} \\ \dfrac{-mV_0}{ik\hbar^2} e^{2ika} & 1 - \dfrac{mV_0}{ik\hbar^2} \end{pmatrix}$$

Operators

An operator, Q, acting on a wave function $\psi(\vec{r})$ creates another wave function, $\psi'(\vec{r})$. Such an operator is called a linear operator if for every complex number α_n,

$$Q\left[\alpha_1 \psi_1(\vec{r}) + \alpha_2 \psi_2(\vec{r})\right] = \alpha_1 Q \psi_1(\vec{r}) + \alpha_2 Q \psi_2(\vec{r})$$

The simplest set of operators we'll use are the *spatial operators*, X, Y, and Z which are defined by

$$X\Psi(x,y,z,t) = x\Psi(x,y,z,t)$$
$$Y\Psi(x,y,z,t) = y\Psi(x,y,z,t)$$
$$Z\Psi(x,y,z,t) = z\Psi(x,y,z,t)$$

In other words, a spatial operator acting on a wave function simply returns the value of its coordinate times the wave function.

Perhaps the strangest and most useful set of operators are the *momentum operators*, p_x, p_y, p_z, which are defined by

$$p_x\Psi(x,y,z,t) = \frac{\hbar}{i}\frac{\partial}{\partial x}\Psi(x,y,z,t)$$

$$p_y\Psi(x,y,z,t) = \frac{\hbar}{i}\frac{\partial}{\partial y}\Psi(x,y,z,t)$$

$$p_z\Psi(x,y,z,t) = \frac{\hbar}{i}\frac{\partial}{\partial z}\Psi(x,y,z,t)$$

Note that all the operators we're dealing with must act on some function to their right; therefore, none of these operators should be sitting at the end of an equation.

As in classical mechanics, we have a *hamiltonian* in quantum mechanics; however, in quantum mechanics, the hamiltonian is an operator:

$$H = \frac{p^2}{2m} + V\left(\vec{r},t\right) = \frac{-\hbar^2}{2m}\nabla^2 + V\left(\vec{r},t\right)$$

We will find that for a stationary state, the eigenvalue of the Hamiltonian operator is the energy of the state.

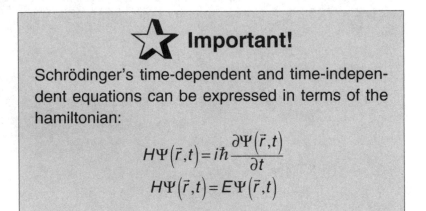

★ Important!

Schrödinger's time-dependent and time-independent equations can be expressed in terms of the hamiltonian:

$$H\Psi\left(\vec{r},t\right) = i\hbar\frac{\partial\Psi\left(\vec{r},t\right)}{\partial t}$$

$$H\Psi\left(\vec{r},t\right) = E\Psi\left(\vec{r},t\right)$$

Every quantity that's measurable in the real world is called an *observable* and is related to a quantum mechanical operator. Unlike classical mechanics, quantum mechanics does not predict definite outcomes to experiments; instead, quantum mechanics can predict the relative likelihood of a variety of possible outcomes. We'll start with a simple and powerful calculation called the *expectation value* of an operator, sometimes referred to as the mean value, though we must carefully understand what it is we're averaging.

Don't Forget!

The expectation value of an operator is *not* the average of a series of measurements performed on a single system. Rather, imagine large number systems that are initially identical, and the expectation value is the result of averaging a *single* measurement on each one of the systems.

Observations on quantum systems *change the system*. Correspondingly, after a measurement, the system has a new state, possibly with a very *different* wave function. Thus a repeated measurement will *not* have the same distribution of possible outcomes that the initial measurement did.

Earlier we learned about the scalar product of vectors. Similarly, we can have scalar products of states, for example,

$$\langle \psi | \psi \rangle \equiv \int \psi^* \psi \, d^3 r = 1$$

is the normalization condition written in terms of the scalar product. We could also have the scalar product of two different states:

$$\langle \psi_2 | \psi_1 \rangle \equiv \int \psi_2^* \psi_1 \, d^3 r$$

The expectation value of an operator, Q, for a system in state ψ is

$$\langle Q \rangle = \langle Q \rangle_\psi = \langle \psi | Q | \psi \rangle = \int \psi^* Q \psi \, d^3 r$$

where some texts may more emphatically group $Q\psi$ together to emphasize that first Q must act on ψ and then the multiplication and integration are carried out. The root-mean-square deviation of the observable Q is defined by

$$\Delta Q = \sqrt{\langle Q^2 \rangle - \langle Q \rangle^2}$$

Solved Problem 3.7 Refer to Solved Problem 3.4. At time $t = 0$ the particle is in the first excited state, $\Psi_2(x, 0) = \psi_2(x)$. Calculate the expectation value of the operators x and p_x.

Solution. Note that the time-dependent wave function is

$$\Psi(x,t) = \sqrt{\frac{2}{a}} \sin\left[2\pi\left(\frac{x}{a} - \frac{1}{2} \right) \right] e^{-iE_2 t/\hbar}$$

Since we started in an eigenstate of energy, we will always be in that energy eigenstate, and there will be no time dependence of expectation values. Therefore we can calculate

$$\langle x \rangle = \int_{-a/2}^{a/2} \psi^* x\psi\, dx = \int_{-a/2}^{a/2} x \frac{2}{a} \sin^2\left[2\pi\left(\frac{x}{a} - \frac{1}{2} \right) \right] dx$$

Although we could carry out this integration, we needn't because the integrand is an odd function being integrated over a symmetric interval, and so the result will be $\langle x \rangle = 0$. This useful trick will also apply to the other expectation value,

$$\langle p_x \rangle = \int_{-a/2}^{a/2} \psi^* \left(\frac{\hbar}{i} \frac{d\psi}{dx} \right) dx = \int_{-a/2}^{a/2} \frac{2\pi\hbar}{ia^2} \sin\left[4\pi\left(\frac{x}{a} - \frac{1}{2} \right) \right] dx$$

since sine is even and cosine is odd, we have $\langle p_x \rangle = 0$.

Solved Problem 3.8 Consider another formulation for the root-mean-square deviation of the operator Q in the normalized state $|\psi\rangle$

$$\Delta Q = \sqrt{\left\langle \left(Q - \langle Q \rangle \right)^2 \right\rangle}$$

(a) Show that this definition is equivalent to that given earlier.

(b) Use this formulation to interpret the term root-mean-square deviation.

Solution.

(a) By the given definition we have

$$\left\langle \left(Q - \langle Q \rangle \right)^2 \right\rangle = \left\langle \psi \left| \left(Q - \langle Q \rangle \right)^2 \right| \psi \right\rangle$$

Note that in this equation $\langle Q \rangle$ is a scalar, short for $\langle Q \rangle \mathbf{1}$ where $\mathbf{1}$ is the identity operator. Hence,

$$\left\langle \left(Q - \langle Q \rangle \right)^2 \right\rangle = \left\langle \psi \left| \left(Q^2 - 2\langle Q \rangle Q + \langle Q \rangle^2 \right) \right| \psi \right\rangle$$

$$\left\langle \left(Q - \langle Q \rangle \right)^2 \right\rangle = \left\langle \psi \left| Q^2 \right| \psi \right\rangle - 2\langle Q \rangle \left\langle \psi \left| Q \right| \psi \right\rangle + \langle Q \rangle^2 \left\langle \psi \middle| \psi \right\rangle$$

Comparing this with the previous definition, we find that the are the same.

(b) The root-mean-square deviation expresses the average of the deviations of Q from its expectation value, $\langle Q \rangle$. It therefore characterizes the dispersion of the measurement results about $\langle Q \rangle$.

Chapter 4
FOUNDATIONS OF QUANTUM MECHANICS

Introduction

In classical mechanics, the position of a particle is described by a vector having three real number elements. Though an analogous description exists in quantum mechanics, there are many significant differences. The state of a quantum mechanical system is described by an element of an abstract vector space called the *state space* and

denoted ε. In Dirac notation, an element of this space is called a *ket* and is denoted by the symbol $|\ \rangle$.

An *observable* is represented by an hermitian operator for which one can find an orthonormal basis of the state space that consists of eigenvectors of the operator. If the state space is finite-dimensional, then any hermitian operator represents an observable. In Dirac notation, an operator is represented by a letter. Since the action of an operator on a vector yields another vector, an expression of the form $Q|\psi\rangle$ also represents a ket.

A *functional* is a mapping from a vector space to the complex field. The *dual space*, ε^*, of the state space ε consists of all linear functionals acting on ε. In Dirac notation, an element of ε^* is called a *bra* and is designated by the symbol $\langle\ |$. We can associate with any ket $|\psi\rangle$ of ε an element $\langle\varphi|$ of ε^*. The action of a bra $\langle\psi|$ on a ket $|\chi\rangle$ is the scalar product, yielding a complex number represented by $\langle\psi|\chi\rangle$.

Consider a subspace ε_m of ε that is spanned by m orthonormal vectors. There is a *projection operator* into this subspace defined by the linear operator

$$P_m = \sum_{i=1}^{m} |\varphi_i\rangle\langle\varphi_i|$$

For example, such an operator could find the projection of an arbitrary vector $|\psi\rangle$ in three-space spanned by the orthonormal vectors $|\varphi_1\rangle$, $|\varphi_2\rangle$, $|\varphi_3\rangle$ into the plane spanned by $|\varphi_1\rangle$, $|\varphi_2\rangle$:

$$P_2|\psi\rangle = |\varphi_1\rangle\big(\langle\varphi_1|\psi\rangle\big) + |\varphi_2\rangle\big(\langle\varphi_2|\psi\rangle\big)$$

An orthonormal set of kets constitutes a basis if and only if it satisfies the *closure relation*,

$$\sum_i |u_i\rangle\langle u_i| = 1$$

or

$$\int |w_\alpha\rangle\langle w_\alpha| \, d\alpha = 1$$

where **1** denotes the identity operator in ε, the $\{|u_i\rangle\}$ are a discrete basis, and the $\{|w_a\rangle\}$ are a continuous basis. Using the notation of the projector onto the space spanned by the set of kets, we can write these relations in an equivalent form: $P\{u_i\} = 1$ or $P\{w_a\} = 1$.

Solved Problem 4.1 Prove that if an orthonormal discrete set of kets $\{|u_i\rangle\}$ constitutes a basis, then it follows that $\sum_i |u_i\rangle\langle u_i| = 1$

Solution. Let $|\psi\rangle$ be an arbitrary ket belonging to the state space. Since $\{|u_i\rangle\}$ is a basis, by definition there exists a unique expansion $|\psi\rangle = \sum_i C_i |u_i\rangle$. We use the orthonormalization relation to obtain

$$\langle u_j | \psi \rangle = \sum_j C_i \langle u_j | u_i \rangle = \sum_j C_i \delta_{ij} = C_j$$

Therefore,

$$|\psi\rangle = \sum_i (C_i)|u_i\rangle = \sum_i (\langle u_i | \psi \rangle)|u_i\rangle = \left[\sum_i |u_i\rangle\langle u_i|\right]|\psi\rangle$$

where we could change the order because $\langle u_i | \psi \rangle$ is a scalar. Since for any ket $|\psi\rangle$ the action of the operator $P\{u_i\}$ yields the same ket, by definition the operator is the identity operator.

Postulates

As emphasized in Chapter 1, the extent of validity of a physical theory is continuously investigated by confronting results calculated by theory with measurements obtained in experiments. In the context of quantum mechanics, the measurement of a physical quantity involves three principle questions.

You Need to Know ✔

What are the possible results in the measurement?
What is the probability of obtaining each of the
    possible results?
What is the state of the system after the
    measurement?

Postulate I: The state of a physical system at time t_0 is defined by specifying a ket $|\psi(t_0)\rangle$ belonging to the state space ε.

Postulate II: A measurable physical quantity Q is described by an observable Q acting on ε.

Postulate III: The possible results in the measurement of a physical quantity are the eigenvalues of the corresponding observable Q.

Postulate IV: Suppose that the system is in a normalized state $|\psi\rangle$, so $\langle\psi|\psi\rangle = 1$. When Q is measured, the probability $P(q_n)$ of obtaining the eigenvalue q_n is

$$P(q_n) = \sum_{i=1}^{g_n} \left| \langle u_n^i | \psi \rangle \right|^2$$

where g_n is the degeneracy of q_n and $|u_n^i\rangle$ form an orthonormal basis of the subspace ε_n that consists of eigenvectors of Q with eigenvalues q_n.

Postulate V: If the measurement of a quantity Q on a physical system in the state $|\psi\rangle$ gives the result q_n, then immediately after the measurement, the state is given by the normalized projection of $|\psi\rangle$ onto the eigenspace ε_n associated with q_n; that is,

$$\frac{P_n|\psi\rangle}{\sqrt{\langle\psi|P_n|\psi\rangle}}$$

Postulate VI: The time evolution of the state vector $|\psi(t)\rangle$ of a physical system is governed by the Schrödinger equation

$$H(t)|\psi(t)\rangle = i\hbar \frac{d|\psi(t)\rangle}{dt}$$

where $H(t)$ is the observable corresponding to the classical hamiltonian of the system.

Solved Problem 4.2 Let $|\psi_1\rangle, |\psi_2\rangle$ be two orthonormal states of a physical system and let Q be an observable of the system. Consider a nondegenerate eigenvalue of Q denoted by q_n to which the normalized state $|\varphi_n\rangle$ corresponds. We define $P_i(q_n) = |\langle \varphi_n | \psi_i \rangle|^2$.

(a) What is the interpretation of $P_i(q_n)$?

(b) A given particle is in the state $3|\psi_1\rangle - 4i|\psi_2\rangle$. What is the probability of obtaining q_n when Q is measured?

Solution.

(a) $P_1(q_n)$ is the probability of obtaining q_n when Q is measured while the system is in the state $|\psi_1\rangle$. The same is the case with $P_2(q_n)$ in the state $|\psi_2\rangle$.

(b) The normalized state of the particle is

$$|\psi\rangle = \frac{3|\psi_1\rangle - 4i|\psi_2\rangle}{\sqrt{9+16}} = \frac{1}{5}\left(3|\psi_1\rangle - 4i|\psi_2\rangle\right)$$

The probability of measuring q_n is

$$P(q_n) = |\langle \varphi_n | \psi \rangle|^2 = \frac{1}{25}|3\langle \varphi_n | \psi_1 \rangle - 4i\langle \varphi_n | \psi_2 \rangle|^2$$

$$P(q_n) = \frac{1}{25}\left[9P_1(q_n) + 16P_2(q_n) + 2\Re\left(12i\langle \varphi_n | \psi_1 \rangle \langle \varphi_n | \psi_2 \rangle^*\right)\right]$$

Solved Problem 4.3 Consider postulate IV introduced in this section and generalize for the case of a continuous spectrum.

Solution. Consider a physical observable Q and suppose that the system is in a normalized state $|\psi\rangle$. Let $|v_\alpha^\beta\rangle$ form an orthonormal basis of the state space consisting of eigenvectors of Q:

$$Q\left|v_\alpha^\beta\right\rangle = \alpha\left|v_\alpha^\beta\right\rangle$$

The index β distinguishes between eigenvectors corresponding to the same degenerate eigenvalue α of Q. This index can be either discrete or continuous, and we assume that it is continuous and varies in the domain $B(\alpha)$. Since the spectrum of Q is continuous, it is meaningless to speak about the probability of obtaining an eigenvalue α. Instead, we should speak about the differential probability, $dP(\alpha)$, of obtaining a result between α and $\alpha + d\alpha$. In analogy to postulate IV, we then have

$$dP(\alpha) = \left[\int_{B(\alpha)}\left|\left\langle v_\alpha^\beta \middle| \psi \right\rangle\right|^2 d\beta\right] d\alpha$$

Properties of Operators

Consider two operators, A and B. In general, the expressions AB and BA are not identical—multiplication of operators is *not commutative*. An important concept in quantum mechanics is the *commutator*, $[A, B]$, of two operators defined by

$$[A, B] = AB - BA$$

If $[A, B] = 0$, then A and B are called *commuting operators*. A set of observables is called a complete set of commuting observables if all sub-pairs commute, in which case there exists a unique orthonormal basis of common eigenvectors.

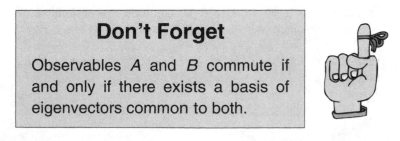

Don't Forget

Observables *A* and *B* commute if and only if there exists a basis of eigenvectors common to both.

Commutivity of operators has an important relationship to the measurement of the observables they correspond to. In quantum mechanics, making a measurement forces the system to assume a state that is an eigenvector of whatever observable was measured. If a second measurement of a *different but commuting observable* is immediately made, the state of the system will remain the same eigenvector.

Just as a function of a variable x can be expanded in a power series in x, $F(x) = \sum_{n=1}^{\infty} a_n x^n$, the corresponding function of an operator can be defined by a series that has the same coefficients:

$$F(A) = \sum_{n=1}^{\infty} a_n A^n$$

The *adjoint* or *hermitian conjugate* of an operator A is denoted by $A^{\dagger}$. For every $|\varphi\rangle$ and $|\psi\rangle$, we have $\langle\psi|A^{\dagger}|\varphi\rangle = \langle\varphi|A|\psi\rangle^*$. An inspection of this and the statements in Chapter 2 shows that in order to obtain the hermitian conjugate of any expression, it suffices to apply the following procedure:

You Need to Know ✔

Replace the constants by their complex conjugates.

Replace the kets by the bras associated with them.

Replace the bras by the kets associated with them.

Replace the operators by their adjoint operators.

Reverse the order of the factors.

For example, $(\lambda\langle\varphi|AB|\psi\rangle)^{\dagger} = \lambda^*\langle\psi|B^{\dagger}A^{\dagger}|\varphi\rangle$, where the position of the constant doesn't matter, so it was kept in front.

Solved Problem 4.4 Prove that for operators A, B, and C, the following identities are valid:

(a) $[B,A] = -[A,B]$

(b) $[A + B,C] = [A,C] + [B,C]$

(c) $[A,BC] = [A,B]C + B[A,C]$.

Solution.

(a) $[B,A] = BA - AB = -(AB - BA) = -[A,B]$

(b) $[A + B,C] = (A + B)C - C(A + B) = AC + BC - CA - CB$

Rearranging and regrouping these we find

$$[A + B,C] = (AC - CA) + (BC - CB) = [A,C] + [B,C]$$

(c) $[A, BC] = ABC - BCA = ABC + 0 - BCA$ where we want to insert zero in a useful form:

$$[A, BC] = (ABC - BAC) + (BAC - BCA) = [A,B]C + B[A,C]$$

Representations

When a basis is chosen in the abstract state space, each ket, bra, and operator can be characterized by specifying its coordinates for that basis. We say that the abstract object is *represented* by the corresponding set of numbers, and using these numbers, the prescribed calculations are performed. Choosing a representation means choosing an orthonormal basis in the state space.

In a discrete basis, $\{|u_i\rangle\}$, a ket $|\psi\rangle$ is represented by the set of numbers $C_i = \langle u_i|\psi\rangle$. These numbers can be arranged vertically to form a column matrix:

$$(C_i) = \begin{pmatrix} C_1 \\ C_2 \\ \cdot \\ \cdot \\ \cdot \end{pmatrix}$$

A bra $\langle\varphi|$ is represented by the set of numbers $b_i^* = \langle\varphi|u_i\rangle$, which are the complex conjugates of the components of the ket $|\varphi\rangle$ associated with $\langle\varphi|$. These numbers can be arranged horizontally to form a row matrix, $(b_1^* \ b_2^* \cdots)$.

In a continuous basis, $\{|w_\alpha\rangle\}$, kets and bras are represented by a continuous infinity of numbers, that is, by a function of α. A ket, $|\psi\rangle$, is represented by the set of numbers $C(\alpha) = \langle w_\alpha|\psi\rangle$, and a bra, $\langle\varphi|$, is represented by $b^*(\alpha) = \langle\varphi|w_\alpha\rangle$.

Once a representation is chosen, we can use the components of the ket and the bra to calculate the scalar product:

$$\langle\varphi|\psi\rangle = \sum_i b_i^* C_i$$

or

$$\langle\varphi|\psi\rangle = \int b^*(\alpha) C(\alpha) \, d\alpha$$

An operator is represented by the numbers

$$A_{ij} = \langle u_i | A | u_j \rangle$$

or

$$A(\alpha, \alpha') = \langle w_\alpha | A | w_{\alpha'} \rangle$$

which in the discrete case can be arranged into a square matrix:

$$[A_{ij}] = \begin{pmatrix} A_{11} & A_{12} & \cdots \\ A_{21} & A_{22} & \cdots \\ \vdots & \vdots & A_{ij} \end{pmatrix}$$

Don't Forget!

For hermitian operators, the diagonal elements are always real numbers since $A^\dagger = A$ implies that $A_{ij} = A_{ji}^*$.

When the representation of a bra, ket, or operator is known in one basis, we can use a simple method to obtain its representation in a different basis. For simplicity, assume that we perform a transformation from one discrete orthonormal basis, $\{|u_i\rangle\}$, to another, $\{|v_i\rangle\}$. The *transformation matrix* is defined by

$$S_{ik} = \langle u_i | v_k \rangle$$
$$(S^\dagger)_{ki} = \langle v_k | u_i \rangle$$

To pass from the components of a ket $|\psi\rangle$ represented in one basis to another, one applies the relation

$$\langle v_k | \psi \rangle = \sum_i \left(S^\dagger \right)_{ki} \langle u_i | \psi \rangle$$

or

$$\langle u_i | \psi \rangle = \sum_k S_{ik} \langle v_k | \psi \rangle$$

The *matrix elements* of an operator A transform as

$$\langle v_k | A | v_l \rangle = \sum_{i,j} \left(S^\dagger \right)_{ki} \langle u_i | A | u_j \rangle S_{jl}$$
$$\langle u_i | A | u_j \rangle = \sum_{k,l} S_{ik} \langle v_k | A | v_l \rangle \left(S^\dagger \right)_{lj}$$

For every ket $|\varphi\rangle$ there corresponds a bra $\langle\varphi|$. The converse is not necessarily true; there are bras with no corresponding kets. Nevertheless, in addition to the vectors belonging to ε, we shall use generalized kets whose norm is not finite. At the same time, however, the scalar product of these kets with every ket is finite. The generalized kets do not represent physical states; they serve to help us analyze and interpret physical states that are represented by kets belonging to ε.

Consider the physical system of a single particle. Together with the state space of the system, we introduce another vector space, called the *wave function space*, denoted by F. This space consists of complex functions of the coordinates (x, y, z) such that the functions $\psi(\vec{r})$ are defined everywhere, continuous, and infinitely differentiable and $\psi(\vec{r})$ must be square integrable. To every function $\psi(\vec{r})$ belonging to F, there corresponds a ket $|\psi\rangle$ belonging to ε. Using the wave functions $\varphi(\vec{r})$ and $\psi(\vec{r})$, we define their scalar product

$$\langle \varphi | \psi \rangle = \int \varphi^* (\vec{r}) \psi (\vec{r}) d^3 r$$

Consider two particular bases of F denoted $\{\xi_{r_0}(\vec{r})\}$ and $\{v_{p_0}(\vec{r})\}$. These bases are not composed of functions belonging to F:

$$\xi_{r_0} (\vec{r}) = \delta (\vec{r} - \vec{r}_0)$$
$$v_{p_0} (\vec{r}) = (2\pi\hbar)^{-3/2} e^{i\vec{p}_0 \cdot \vec{r}/\hbar}$$

To each $\xi_{r_0}(\vec{r})$ we associate a generalized ket denoted by $|\vec{r}_0\rangle$, and similarly for $v_{p_0}(\vec{r})$ we associate a generalized ket $|\vec{p}_0\rangle$. The sets $\{|\vec{r}_0\rangle\}$ and $\{|\vec{p}_0\rangle\}$ constitute orthonormal bases in ε:

$$\langle r_0 | r_0{}' \rangle = \delta (r_0 - r_0{}')$$
$$\int |r_0\rangle\langle r_0| d^3 r = 1$$
$$\langle p_0 | p_0{}' \rangle = \delta (p_0 - p_0{}')$$
$$\int |p_0\rangle\langle p_0| d^3 p = 1$$

We obtain two representations in the state space of a (spinless) particle. The correspondence between the ket $|\psi\rangle$ and the wave function associated with it is given by

$$\psi(\vec{r}_0) = \langle \vec{r}_0 | \psi \rangle$$
$$\bar{\psi}(\vec{p}_0) = \langle \vec{p}_0 | \psi \rangle$$

where $\bar{\psi}(\vec{p}_0)$ is the Fourier transform of $\psi(\vec{r}_0)$. The value of the wave function at the point $\vec{r}$ is the component of the ket $|\psi\rangle$ on the basis vector $|\vec{r}\rangle$ of the $|\vec{r}\rangle$ -representation, and similarly for the Fourier transform.

Exchanging between the $|\vec{r}\rangle$ -representation and the $|\vec{p}\rangle$ -representation is accomplished analogously to the case of continuous bases.

Remember!

$$\langle \vec{r}|\vec{p}\rangle = \langle \vec{p}|\vec{r}\rangle^{*} = (2\pi\hbar)^{-3/2}\, e^{i\vec{p}\cdot\vec{r}/\hbar}$$

$$\psi(\vec{r}) = \langle \vec{r}|\psi\rangle = \int\langle \vec{r}|\vec{p}\rangle\langle \vec{p}|\psi\rangle d^{3}p = (2\pi\hbar)^{-3/2}\int e^{i\vec{p}\cdot\vec{r}/\hbar}\overline{\psi}(\vec{p})d^{3}p$$

$$\overline{\psi}(\vec{p}) = \langle \vec{p}|\psi\rangle = \int\langle \vec{p}|\vec{r}\rangle\langle \vec{r}|\psi\rangle d^{3}r = (2\pi\hbar)^{-3/2}\int e^{-i\vec{p}\cdot\vec{r}/\hbar}\psi(\vec{r})d^{3}r$$

Let $|\psi\rangle$ be a ket belonging to the state space and let $\psi(\vec{r}) = \psi(x,y,z)$ $= \langle \vec{r}|\psi\rangle$ be its corresponding wave function. The three observables X, Y, Z are defined by their action in the $|\vec{r}\rangle$-representation:

$$\langle \vec{r}|X|\psi\rangle = x\langle \vec{r}|\psi\rangle$$

and similarly for the other two components. The operators X, Y, Z are considered to be the components of a vector operator $\vec{R}$. Similarly the operators P_x, P_y, P_z are the components of the vector operator $\vec{P}$, and they are defined by their action in the $|\vec{p}\rangle$-representation, for example:

$$\langle \vec{p}|P_x|\psi\rangle = p_x\langle \vec{p}|\psi\rangle$$

The observables $\vec{R}$ and $\vec{P}$ are of fundamental importance in quantum mechanics. Their commutation relations are called the *canonical commutation relations*.

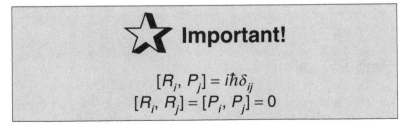

☆ Important!

$$[R_i, P_j] = i\hbar\delta_{ij}$$
$$[R_i, R_j] = [P_i, P_j] = 0$$

Quantization rules are the method for obtaining the quantum mechanics analog of a classical quantity. Consider a system of a single particle. The observables (X, Y, Z) are associated with the coordinates $(x, y,$

z) of the particle; the observables (P_x, P_y, P_z) are associated with the momentum (p_x, p_y, p_z). We shall often use the notation $\vec{R}$ and $\vec{P}$ for these. In classical mechanics, a physical quantity A related to a particle is expressed in terms of the particle's position vector $\vec{r}$ and the momentum $\vec{p}$. To obtain the corresponding quantum mechanics observable, replace these with $\vec{R}$ and $\vec{P}$. Since the expression is not always hermitian, we apply a symmetrization between $\vec{R}$ and $\vec{P}$ to obtain a hermitian operator. Note that there exist quantum mechanical physical variables that have no classical equivalent, e.g. spin.

Solved Problem 4.5 Prove that $\left\langle \vec{r} \left| \vec{P} \right| \psi \right\rangle = \dfrac{\hbar}{i} \nabla \left\langle \vec{r} \middle| \psi \right\rangle$.

Solution. Consider, for example, the x-component (the y- and z-components can be treated in a completely analogous way):

$$\left\langle \vec{r} \left| P_x \right| \psi \right\rangle = \int \left\langle \vec{r} \middle| \vec{p} \right\rangle \left\langle \vec{p} \left| P_x \right| \psi \right\rangle d^3 p$$

where we use the closure relation of the $\left| \vec{p} \right\rangle$ -representation.

$$\left\langle \vec{r} \left| P_x \right| \psi \right\rangle = \left(2\pi\hbar \right)^{-3/2} \int e^{i \vec{p} \cdot \vec{r}/\hbar} p_x \bar{\psi} \left(\vec{p} \right) d^3 p$$

This expression is the Fourier transform of $p_x \bar{\psi}(\vec{p})$ which is $\dfrac{h}{i} \dfrac{\partial}{\partial x} \psi(\vec{r})$. We therefore have

$$\left\langle \vec{r} \left| P_x \right| \psi \right\rangle = \dfrac{\hbar}{i} \dfrac{\partial}{\partial x} \psi(\vec{r})$$

Time Evolution

Since the Schrödinger equation is first-order in time, it follows that if an initial state $\left| \psi(t_0) \right\rangle$ is given, the state $\left| \psi(t) \right\rangle$ is determined; therefore, the time evolution is deterministic. Note that indeterminacy appears only when a physical quantity is measured. The norm of the state vector remains constant, which means that the total probability of finding the particle is conserved.

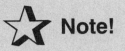

Note!

A physical system is *conservative* if its hamiltonian does not depend explicitly on time.

In classical mechanics, the most important consequence of such an observation is the conservation of energy. Similarly, in quantum mechanics a conservative system possesses important properties that we will frequently exploit in this book.

The time evolution of a conservative system can be found simply by expanding the initial state in the basis of eigenvectors of the (time-independent) hamiltonian:

$$\left| \psi\left(t_0\right) \right\rangle = \sum_n \sum_k a_{nk}\left(t_0\right) \left| \varphi_{nk} \right\rangle$$

where $a_{nk}(t_0) = \langle \varphi_{nk} | \psi(t_0) \rangle$. To obtain the state at later times, multiply each coefficient by $e^{-iE_n(t-t_0)/\hbar}$ where E_n is the eigenvalue of H associated with the state $|\varphi_{nk}\rangle$:

$$\left| \psi\left(t\right) \right\rangle = \sum_n \sum_k a_{nk}\left(t_0\right) e^{-iE_n\left(t-t_0\right)/\hbar} \left| \varphi_{nk} \right\rangle$$

This procedure can be generalized to the case of the continuous spectrum of H, so

$$\left| \psi\left(t\right) \right\rangle = \sum_k \int a_k\left(E,t_0\right) e^{-iE_n\left(t-t_0\right)/\hbar} \left| \varphi_{Ek} \right\rangle dE$$

The eigenstates of H are called stationary states.

Let $|\psi(t)\rangle$ be the normalized ket describing the time evolution of a physical system. The time evolution of the expectation value of an observable Q is governed by the equation

$$\frac{d\langle Q \rangle}{dt} = \frac{1}{i\hbar}\langle [Q,H] \rangle + \left\langle \frac{\partial Q}{\partial t} \right\rangle$$

By definition, a constant of the motion is an observable Q that does not depend explicitly on time and commutes with the hamiltonian.

Uncertainty Relations

As we have seen in previous sections, the position of momentum of a particle in quantum mechanics is not characterized by a single number but rather by a continuous function. By the uncertainty of the position (or momentum) of a particle, we mean the degree of dispersion of the wave function relative to a central value. This quantity can be given a rigorous definition.

The Heisenberg uncertainty principles give lower limits for the product of the uncertainties of the position and corresponding component of momentum of a particle:

$$\Delta r_i \Delta p_i \geq \frac{\hbar}{2}$$

For the case of a conservative system, there is also a relation between the uncertainty of time Δt at which the system evolves to an appreciable extent and the uncertainty of the energy:

$$\Delta t \Delta E \geq \frac{\hbar}{2}$$

The Schrödinger and Heisenberg Pictures

In the formalism described in the previous sections, we considered the time-independent operators that correspond to the observables of the system. The time evolution is entirely contained in the state vector $|\psi(t)\rangle$. This approach is called the *Schrödinger picture*. Since the physical predictions in quantum mechanics are expressed by scalar products of bras and kets and by matrix elements of operators, it is possible to introduce a different formalism for the time evolution. This formalism is called the *Heisenberg picture*. In this formalism, the state of the system is described by a ket that does not vary over time $|\psi_H(t)\rangle = |\psi(t_0)\rangle$. The observables corresponding to physical quantities evolve over time as

$$Q_H(t) = U^\dagger(t,t_0) Q_S U(t,t_0)$$

where Q_S is the observable in the Schrödinger picture and

$$U(t,t_0) = e^{-iH_S(t - t_0)/\hbar}$$

This operator, $U(t,t_0)$, is a unitary operator called the *time evolution operator*. Note that this operator also describes the time evolution of the state vector in the Schrödinger picture:

$$|\psi_S(t)\rangle = U(t,t_0)|\psi_S(t_0)\rangle$$

Chapter 5
THE HARMONIC OSCILLATOR

Introduction

Consider a particle moving under the *harmonic oscillator potential*,

$$V(x) = \frac{1}{2} k x^2$$

Many problems in physics can be approximated by a harmonic oscillator under appropriate conditions. For example, in classical physics we expand a potential around a classical equilibrium point to second order, and we obtain the harmonic potential.

The hamiltonian for the one-dimensional harmonic oscillator is

$$H = \frac{p^2}{2m} + \frac{kx^2}{2}$$

where $k = m\omega^2$. The variables ω and m are, respectively, the angular frequency and the mass of the oscillator. Inserting the quantum mechanical operators, we find the stationary Schrödinger equation is

$$\frac{-\hbar^2}{2m}\frac{d^2\psi(x)}{dx^2} + \frac{m\omega^2}{2}x^2\psi(x) = E\psi(x)$$

The eigenfunctions that are the solutions of the Schrödinger equation for the harmonic oscillator are

$$\psi_n(x) = \sqrt[4]{\frac{1}{\pi\lambda^2}}\frac{1}{\sqrt{2^n n!}}H_n\left(\frac{x}{\lambda}\right)e^{-x^2/2\lambda^2}$$

where $\lambda = \sqrt{\hbar/m\omega}$ and $H_n(\zeta)$ are the *Hermite polynomials*. The eigenenergies of the harmonic oscillator are

$$E_n = \left(n + \frac{1}{2}\right)\hbar\omega \text{ where } n = 0,1,2,...$$

Solved Problem 5.1

(a) Solve the stationary Schrödinger equation for the harmonic oscillator potential and find the stationary eigenstates for this system.

(b) Find the energy eigenvalues of the harmonic oscillator. What is the minimum energy eigenvalue?

Solution.

(a) To simplify notation we define $\varepsilon = \dfrac{2E}{\hbar\omega}$ and perform a change of variables to $\zeta = \sqrt{\dfrac{m\omega}{\hbar}}x$ which shortens the stationary Schrödinger equation to

$$\frac{d^2\psi}{d\zeta^2} + \left(\varepsilon - \zeta^2\right)\psi = 0$$

For large ζ (large x) the dominant part of this differential equation is

$$\frac{d^2\psi}{d\zeta^2} - \zeta^2\psi = 0$$

which suggests that the asymptotic behavior of the wave function is:

$$\psi(\zeta) \sim e^{-\zeta^2/2}$$

We then assume that the full wave function is the product of this asymptotic term and some other term that's yet to be determined:

$$\psi(\zeta) = H(\zeta)e^{-\zeta^2/2}$$

When this is substituted into the differential equation and simplified, we obtain the *Hermite differential equation*:

$$\frac{d^2H(\zeta)}{d\zeta^2} - 2\zeta\frac{dH(\zeta)}{d\zeta} + (\varepsilon - 1)H(\zeta) = 0$$

In order to solve this equation, assume that $H(\zeta)$ can be expanded in a power series, $\sum\limits_{n=0}^{\infty} a_n\zeta^n$, which, when substituted in, yields:

$$\sum_{n=0}^{\infty}\left[a_{n+2}(n+2)(n+1) - 2na_n + (\varepsilon - 1)a_n\right]\zeta^n = 0$$

So we either have the uninteresting case of no solution or every coefficient must be equal to zero:

$$a_{n+2} = \frac{2n - \varepsilon + 1}{(n+2)(n+1)}a_n$$

So if we knew the first two coefficients, a_0, a_1, then we could determine the whole series. However, remember that for large x (and large ζ, we already had the asymptotic behavior we wanted, so this recursion series must terminate at some highest a. The normalization condition for the wave function can be used to determine a_0, a_1.

(b) Use the fact that for some n, the series must terminate, making the numerator of the recursion formula zero:

$$2n + 1 - \varepsilon = 0$$

Now put back in the value of ε and solve for the energy:

$$E_n = \left(n + \frac{1}{2} \right) \hbar\omega$$

The lowest energy, then, is $\hbar\omega/2$.

⭐ Note!

Hermite polynomials are polynomials of degree n that are symmetric for even n and antisymmetric for odd n. The orthogonality relation for Hermite polynomials is

$$\int_{-\infty}^{\infty} e^{-x^2} H_m(x) H_n(x)\, dx = \sqrt{\pi}\, 2^n n!\, \delta_{mn}$$

The first three Hermite polynomials are

$$H_0(x) = 1$$
$$H_1(x) = 2x$$
$$H_2(x) = 4x^2 - 2$$

Higher-Dimensional Harmonic Oscillators

Extending to more dimensions simply entails appropriate addition of other components of p and ω, as demonstrated here for two dimensions:

$$H_2 = \frac{p_x^2 + p_y^2}{2m} + \frac{m}{2}\left(\omega_x^2 x^2 + \omega_y^2 y^2 \right)$$

This is separable into two one-dimensional harmonic oscillators,

$$\psi_{n_x n_y}(x,y) = \psi_{n_x}(x)\psi_{n_y}(y)$$

and the energies simply add,

$$E_{n_x n_y} = \hbar\omega_x \left(n_x + \frac{1}{2} \right) + \hbar\omega_y \left(n_y + \frac{1}{2} \right)$$

so there is no new work. Notice, however, that there can now be *degeneracies*; that is, there could be different combinations of the quantum numbers, n_x, n_y, giving the same energy.

The generalization to three dimensions is similarly straightforward.

Solved Problem 5.2 Find the eigenfunctions and eigenvalues of a two-dimensional isotropic harmonic oscillator and find the degeneracy of the energy levels.

Solution. We begin with the Schrödinger equation:

$$\frac{-\hbar^2}{2m}\left(\frac{\partial^2 \psi(x,y)}{\partial x^2} + \frac{\partial^2 \psi(x,y)}{\partial y^2} \right) + \frac{m\omega^2}{2}\left(x^2 + y^2 \right)\psi(x,y) = E\psi(x,y)$$

When we plug in the wave function with variables separated, the y part is unaffected by the x derivatives and vice versa, and if we divide through by the separated wave function, we can shift all the x parts to one side of the equation and y parts to the other:

$$\frac{-\hbar^2}{2m\psi(x)}\frac{d^2\psi(x)}{dx^2} + \frac{m\omega^2}{2}x^2 - E_x = \frac{\hbar^2}{2m\psi(y)}\frac{d^2\psi(y)}{dy^2} - \frac{m\omega^2}{2}y^2 + E_y$$

Clearly each side of this equation can be separately solved exactly as the one-dimensional case, yielding

$$\sqrt[4]{\frac{1}{\pi\lambda^2}}\frac{1}{\sqrt{2^{n_x} n_x!}}H_{n_x}\left(\frac{x}{\lambda} \right)e^{-x^2/2\lambda^2}\left[\sqrt[4]{\frac{1}{\pi\lambda^2}}\frac{1}{\sqrt{2^{n_y} n_y!}}H_{n_y}\left(\frac{y}{\lambda} \right)e^{-y^2/2\lambda^2} \right]$$

for the eigenfunctions and

$$E = E_x + E_y = (n_x + n_y + 1)\hbar\omega$$

for the eigenenergies. Notice that the lowest possible energy (the *ground state*) is now $\hbar\omega$ and this occurs only when both n_x, n_y are zero, so it has degeneracy 1. The next lowest energy (the *first excited state*), $2\hbar\omega$, occurs when either n_x or n_y is one and the other is zero, so it has degeneracy two, and so on.

Operator Methods for Harmonic Oscillators

Eigenfunctions can be thought of as an orthonormal basis of unit vectors in an n-dimensional vector space obtained by solving the Schrödinger equation. Here we will go one step further—we will find the eigenvalue spectrum and eigenfunctions using operators alone. The *raising and lowering operators* are

$$a_\pm = \frac{1}{\sqrt{2\hbar m\omega}}\left(m\omega x \mp ip\right)$$

Note that the hamiltonian of the harmonic oscillator can be written

$$H = \hbar\omega\left(a_+ a_- + \frac{1}{2}\right)$$

$$H = \hbar\omega\left(a_- a_+ - \frac{1}{2}\right)$$

The commutation relations for these operators are

$$[a_-, a_+] = 1$$
$$[H, a_-] = -\hbar\omega a_-$$
$$[H, a_+] = \hbar\omega a_+$$

Let us denote the nth state of the harmonic oscillator as $|n\rangle$, then

$$a_- |n\rangle = \sqrt{n}\,|n-1\rangle$$
$$a_+ |n\rangle = \sqrt{n+1}\,|n+1\rangle$$

We can now build any state by applying the raising operator to the ground state

$$|n\rangle = \frac{1}{\sqrt{n!}}(a_+)^n |0\rangle$$

where $|0\rangle$ is the lowest energy, or ground state.

Solved Problem 5.3 For the one-dimensional harmonic oscillator,

(a) compute the commutation relations for the raising and lowering operators using $[x,p] = i\hbar$

(b) compute $a_-|n\rangle$ and $a_+|n\rangle$.

Solution.

(a) From the definition of the commutator and the operators we have

$$[a_-,a_+] = \frac{1}{2\hbar m\omega}\left[(m\omega x + ip)(m\omega x - ip) - (m\omega x - ip)(m\omega x + ip)\right]$$

$$[a_-,a_+] = \frac{1}{2\hbar m\omega}\left[(m\omega x)^2 (0) + p^2 (0) + im\omega(px - xp - xp + px)\right]$$

$$[a_-,a_+] = \frac{1}{\hbar}\left[i(px - xp)\right] = \frac{1}{i\hbar}[x,p] = 1$$

$$[H,a_-] = \hbar\omega\left(a_-a_+ - \frac{1}{2}\right)a_- - a_-\hbar\omega\left(a_-a_+ - \frac{1}{2}\right)$$

$$[H,a_-] = \hbar\omega(a_-a_+a_- - a_-a_-a_+) = -\hbar\omega a_-\left[a_-,a_+\right] = -\hbar\omega a_-$$

$$[H,a_+] = \hbar\omega\left(a_-a_+ - \frac{1}{2}\right)a_+ - a_+\hbar\omega\left(a_-a_+ - \frac{1}{2}\right)$$

$$[H,a_+] = \hbar\omega(a_-a_+a_+ - a_+a_-a_+) = \hbar\omega\left[a_-,a_+\right]a_+ = \hbar\omega a_+$$

(b) Use the two definitions of the hamiltonian operator and the energy eigenvalues from earlier

$$H|n\rangle = \hbar\omega\left(a_+a_- + \frac{1}{2}\right)|n\rangle = \hbar\omega\left(n + \frac{1}{2}\right)|n\rangle$$

which tells us that $a_+a_-|n\rangle = n|n\rangle$ and

$$H|n\rangle = \hbar\omega\left(a_-a_+ - \frac{1}{2}\right)|n\rangle = \hbar\omega\left(n + \frac{1}{2}\right)|n\rangle$$

which tells us that $a_-a_+|n\rangle = (n+1)|n\rangle$. Now exploit our results from part (a)

$$a_+ = \frac{1}{\hbar\omega}[H, a_+]$$

$$a_- = \frac{-1}{\hbar\omega}[H, a_-]$$

to determine the result of just one of these raising or lowering operators acting on an energy eigenstate.

$$a_+|n\rangle = \frac{1}{\hbar\omega}[H, a_+]|n\rangle = \frac{1}{\hbar\omega}\left\{H(a_+|n\rangle) - a_+\left[\hbar\omega\left(n + \frac{1}{2}\right)\right]|n\rangle\right\}$$

Rearranging this to solve for $H(a_+|n\rangle)$ we find

$$H(a_+|n\rangle) = \hbar\omega a_+|n\rangle + a_+\left[\hbar\omega\left(n + \frac{1}{2}\right)\right]|n\rangle = \hbar\omega\left(n + \frac{3}{2}\right)(a_+|n\rangle)$$

This tells us that $a_+|n\rangle$ is proportional to $|n+1\rangle$, so we will define

$$a_+|n\rangle = \alpha_+|n + 1\rangle$$

and similarly

$$a_+|n\rangle = \alpha_-|n - 1\rangle$$

These proportionality constants can be determined using

$$\langle n + 1|n + 1\rangle = \langle n|a_-a_+|n\rangle = \alpha_+^2$$
$$\langle n - 1|n - 1\rangle = \langle n|a_+a_-|n\rangle = \alpha_-^2$$

since the $|n\rangle$ are normalized states and $(a_+)^\dagger = a_-$. Using our earlier results for $a_- a_+ |n\rangle$, we find that

$$a_+ |n\rangle = \sqrt{n+1}\,|n+1\rangle$$
$$a_- |n\rangle = \sqrt{n}\,|n-1\rangle$$

Notice that at the bottom of the ladder, this automatically gives us

$$a_- |0\rangle = 0$$

Solved Problem 5.4 Compute the matrix elements of the operators x and p for the one-dimensional harmonic oscillator.

Solution. Let the eigenfunctions be $\varphi_n(x)$ so we can write

$$x_{nk} = \langle n|x|k\rangle = \int_{-\infty}^{\infty} \varphi_n^*(x)\, x \varphi_k(x)\, dx$$

$$p_{nk} = \langle n|p|k\rangle = \int_{-\infty}^{\infty} \varphi_n^*(x)\, p \varphi_k(x)\, dx$$

and do as much of the problem as possible using the raising and lowering operators:

$$x = \sqrt{\frac{\hbar}{2m\omega}}\,(a_+ + a_-)$$

$$p = i\sqrt{\frac{m\omega\hbar}{2}}\,(a_+ - a_-)$$

We can now compute

$$\langle n|x|k\rangle = \sqrt{\frac{\hbar}{2m\omega}}\,\langle n|(a_+ + a_-)|k\rangle = \sqrt{\frac{\hbar}{2m\omega}}\left(\sqrt{k+1}\,\delta_{n,k+1} + \sqrt{k}\,\delta_{n,k-1}\right)$$

so that

$$\langle n|x|k\rangle = \begin{cases} \sqrt{\dfrac{\hbar(n+1)}{2m\omega}} & \text{for } k = n+1 \\[2ex] \sqrt{\dfrac{\hbar n}{2m\omega}} & \text{for } k = n-1 \\[2ex] 0 & \text{otherwise} \end{cases}$$

In the same way we find

$$\langle n|p|k\rangle = i\sqrt{\frac{m\omega\hbar}{2}}\,\langle n|(a_+ - a_-)|k\rangle = i\sqrt{\frac{m\omega\hbar}{2}}\left(\sqrt{k+1}\,\delta_{n,k+1} - \sqrt{k}\,\delta_{n,k-1}\right)$$

We could write the result in the same format as above, but for variety, we will instead express it as a matrix:

$$\langle n|p|k\rangle = i\sqrt{\frac{m\omega\hbar}{2}}\begin{pmatrix} 0 & -1 & 0 & 0 & \cdot & \cdot & \cdot \\ 1 & 0 & -\sqrt{2} & 0 & \cdot & \cdot & \cdot \\ 0 & \sqrt{2} & 0 & -\sqrt{3} & \cdot & \cdot & \cdot \\ 0 & 0 & \sqrt{3} & 0 & \cdot & \cdot & \cdot \\ \cdot & \cdot & \cdot & \cdot & \cdot & \cdot & \cdot \\ \cdot & \cdot & \cdot & \vdots & \cdot & \cdot & \cdot \\ \cdot & \cdot & \cdot & \cdot & \cdot & \cdot & \cdot \end{pmatrix}$$

Chapter 6
ANGULAR MOMENTUM

Commutation Relations

As in classical mechanics, we introduce the *angular momentum*, $\vec{L} = \vec{r} \times \vec{p}$, with Cartesian representation, $\vec{L} = (L_x, L_y, L_z)$. Thus, for example,

$$L_x = yp_z - zp_y = \frac{\hbar}{i}\left(y\frac{\partial}{\partial z} - z\frac{\partial}{\partial y} \right)$$

The commutation relations are most conveniently expressed using the *Levi-Civita symbol*

$$\varepsilon_{ijk} = \begin{cases} 1 & ijk \text{ have cyclic permutation} \\ -1 & ijk \text{ have anticyclic permutation} \\ 0 & \text{otherwise} \end{cases}$$

In Cartesian coordinates with $i,j,k = x,y,z$,

$$\left[L_i, L_j\right] = i\hbar \sum_k \varepsilon_{ijk} L_k$$

$$\left[L_i, r_j\right] = i\hbar \sum_k \varepsilon_{ijk} r_k$$

$$\left[L_i, p_j\right] = i\hbar \sum_k \varepsilon_{ijk} p_k$$

The magnitude of these operators does commute with the components:

$$\left[L^2, \vec{L}\right] = 0$$

$$\left[L_i, r^2\right] = 0$$

$$\left[L_i, p^2\right] = 0$$

Solved Problem 6.1 Prove that $\left[L_i, r_j\right] = i\hbar \sum_k \varepsilon_{ijk} r_k$.

Solution. We can express L_i in terms of r and p using $L_i = \sum_{k,l} \varepsilon_{kli} r_k p_l$; thus

$$\left[L_i, r_j\right] = \left[\sum_{k,l} \varepsilon_{kli} r_k p_l, r_j\right] = \sum_{k,l} \varepsilon_{kli} \left(r_k \left[p_l, r_j\right] + \left[r_k, r_j\right] p_l\right)$$

and since $[r_k, r_j] = 0$ and $[p_l, r_j] = i\hbar\delta_{lj}$, we obtain

$$\left[L_i, r_j\right] = \sum_{k,l} \varepsilon_{kli} r_k \left(-i\hbar\delta_{lj}\right) = -i\hbar \sum_k \varepsilon_{kji} r_k = i\hbar \sum_k \varepsilon_{ijk} r_k$$

Raising and Lowering Operators

We define the *raising and lowering operators for angular momentum* as

$$L_\pm = L_x \pm iL_y$$

These are not hermitian operators since $L_+ = L_-^\dagger$. We call them raising and lowering operators because when applied to an eigenfunction of L_z, the former raises the eigenvalue by $\hbar$ and the latter lowers it by $\hbar$. The commutation relations of these are

$$\left[L^2, L_\pm\right] = 0$$
$$\left[L_z, L_\pm\right] = \pm\hbar L_\pm$$
$$\left[L_+, L_-\right] = 2\hbar L_z$$

It is also useful to know that

$$L_\pm L_\mp = L^2 - L_z^2 \pm \hbar L_z$$

These raising and lowering operators allow us to represent all the eigenfunctions of L^2 and L_z using only one eigenfunction and the operators $L_\pm$.

Since the operators L^2 and L_z represent physical quantities, they must be hermitian operators, and since they also commute, it must be possible to find simultaneous eigenfunctions, $\{|\ell,m\rangle\}$, which comprise a complete orthonormal basis.

Things to Remember

$$L^2|\ell,m\rangle = \ell(\ell+1)\hbar^2|\ell,m\rangle$$
$$L_z|\ell,m\rangle = m\hbar|\ell,m\rangle$$
$$L_\pm|\ell,m\rangle = \sqrt{\ell(\ell+1) - m(m\pm 1)}\hbar|\ell,m\pm 1\rangle$$

Note that if $|\ell,m\rangle$ is an eigenvector of L^2 with eigenvalue $\ell(\ell+1)$, then there are $2(\ell+1)$ possible eigenvalues for L_z:

$$m = -\ell, -\ell + 1, ..., 0, ..., \ell - 1, \ell$$

Therefore

$$L_+|\ell,\ell\rangle = 0$$
$$L_-|\ell,-\ell\rangle = 0$$

which can be exploited to derive some of the statements above.

Solved Problem 6.2 Find the matrix representations of L_x, L_y, L_z, L^2 in the basis of eigenvectors for L^2 and L_z for a system with $\ell = 1$.

Solution. These operators all represent observables, so they are hermitian, as are their matrix representations. Let us call $|1\rangle$ the eigenvector for $\ell = m = 1$, $|0\rangle$ for $\ell = 1$, $m = 0$, and $|-1\rangle$ for $\ell = -m = 1$. To find the matrix representation of L_x, we need to compute the following quantities:

$$L_x|1\rangle = \frac{1}{2}(L_+ + L_-)|1\rangle = \frac{1}{2}L_-|1\rangle = \frac{\hbar}{\sqrt{2}}|0\rangle$$

$$L_x|0\rangle = \frac{1}{2}(L_+ + L_-)|0\rangle = \frac{\hbar}{\sqrt{2}}(|1\rangle + |-1\rangle)$$

$$L_x|-1\rangle = \frac{1}{2}(L_+ + L_-)|-1\rangle = \frac{1}{2}L_+|-1\rangle = \frac{\hbar}{\sqrt{2}}|0\rangle$$

The standard basis is

$$|1\rangle = \begin{pmatrix} 1 \\ 0 \\ 0 \end{pmatrix}$$

$$|0\rangle = \begin{pmatrix} 0 \\ 1 \\ 0 \end{pmatrix}$$

$$|-1\rangle = \begin{pmatrix} 0 \\ 0 \\ 1 \end{pmatrix}$$

and in this basis the matrix representation of L_x is

$$L_x = \frac{\hbar}{\sqrt{2}} \begin{pmatrix} 0 & 1 & 0 \\ 1 & 0 & 1 \\ 0 & 1 & 0 \end{pmatrix}$$

Similarly for L_y we have

$$L_y|1\rangle = \frac{1}{2i}(L_+ - L_-)|1\rangle = \frac{i\hbar}{\sqrt{2}}|0\rangle$$

$$L_y|0\rangle = \frac{1}{2i}(L_+ - L_-)|0\rangle = \frac{i\hbar}{\sqrt{2}}(|1\rangle - |-1\rangle)$$

$$L_y|-1\rangle = \frac{1}{2i}(L_+ - L_-)|-1\rangle = \frac{-i\hbar}{\sqrt{2}}|0\rangle$$

These give the matrix representation of L_y:

$$L_y = \frac{\hbar}{\sqrt{2}} \begin{pmatrix} 0 & -i & 0 \\ i & 0 & -i \\ 0 & i & 0 \end{pmatrix}$$

Since the basis vectors are eigenvectors of L_z, it is easy to see that

$$L_z = \hbar \begin{pmatrix} 1 & 0 & 0 \\ 0 & 0 & 0 \\ 0 & 0 & -1 \end{pmatrix}$$

Using $L^2|\ell,m\rangle = \ell(\ell+1)\hbar^2|\ell,m\rangle$ we see that L^2 is a diagonal matrix with $2\hbar^2$ along the diagonal:

$$L^2 = 2\hbar^2 \begin{pmatrix} 1 & 0 & 0 \\ 0 & 1 & 0 \\ 0 & 0 & 1 \end{pmatrix}$$

Alternatively, we could calculate the sum of the squares of each component of angular momentum:

$$L^2 = \frac{\hbar^2}{2}\begin{pmatrix} 1 & 0 & 1 \\ 0 & 2 & 0 \\ 1 & 0 & 1 \end{pmatrix} + \frac{\hbar^2}{2}\begin{pmatrix} 1 & 0 & -1 \\ 0 & 2 & 0 \\ -1 & 0 & 1 \end{pmatrix} + \hbar^2\begin{pmatrix} 1 & 0 & 0 \\ 0 & 0 & 0 \\ 0 & 0 & 1 \end{pmatrix}$$

$$L^2 = L_x^2 + L_y^2 + L_z^2 = \hbar^2\begin{pmatrix} 2 & 0 & 0 \\ 0 & 2 & 0 \\ 0 & 0 & 2 \end{pmatrix}$$

Differential Representation

The representation of eigenvectors and eigenvalues is often more convenient using spherical coordinates:

$$L_x = \frac{\hbar}{i}\left(-\sin\varphi\,\frac{\partial}{\partial\theta} - \frac{\cos\varphi}{\tan\theta}\frac{\partial}{\partial\varphi}\right)$$

$$L_y = \frac{\hbar}{i}\left(\cos\varphi\,\frac{\partial}{\partial\theta} - \frac{\sin\varphi}{\tan\theta}\frac{\partial}{\partial\varphi}\right)$$

$$L_z = \frac{\hbar}{i}\frac{\partial}{\partial\varphi}$$

$$L^2 = -\hbar^2\left(\frac{\partial^2}{\partial\theta^2} + \cot\theta\,\frac{\partial}{\partial\theta} + \frac{1}{\sin^2\theta}\frac{\partial^2}{\partial\varphi^2}\right),$$

$$L_\pm = \hbar e^{\pm i\varphi}\left(\pm\frac{\partial}{\partial\theta} + i\cot\theta\,\frac{\partial}{\partial\varphi}\right)$$

Here we can clearly see that the eigenvectors of L^2 and L_z are functions that depend on the angles only; hence, we can represent the wave function as

$$\psi(r,\theta,\varphi) = R(r)Y_\ell^m(\theta,\varphi)$$

and solve the radial part separately.

For a *central potential*, $V(\vec{r}) = V(r)$, we find that these angular functions are the *spherical harmonics*

$$|\ell,m\rangle = Y_\ell^m(\theta,\varphi)$$

which can be represented as

$$Y_\ell^m(\theta,\varphi) = \epsilon \sqrt{\frac{(2\ell+1)}{4\pi}\frac{(\ell-|m|)!}{(\ell+|m|)!}} e^{im\varphi} P_\ell^m(\cos\theta)$$

where $\epsilon = (-1)^m$ for $m \geq 0$ and $\epsilon = 1$ for $m \leq 0$. The orthonormalization relation for the spherical harmonics is

$$\int_0^{2\pi} d\varphi \int_0^\pi \left[Y_{\ell'}^{m'}(\theta,\varphi) \right]^* Y_\ell^m(\theta,\varphi) \sin\theta d\theta = \delta_{\ell\ell'}\delta_{mm'}$$

The *associated Legendre functions*, P_ℓ^m, are defined by

$$P_\ell^m(x) = \sqrt{(1-x)^{|m|}} \frac{d^{|m|}}{dx^{|m|}} P_\ell(x)$$

and are solutions to this differential equation:

$$\left[(1-x^2)\frac{d^2}{dx^2} - 2x\frac{d}{dx} + \left(\ell(\ell+1) - \frac{m^2}{1-x^2} \right) \right] P_\ell^m(x) = 0$$

Letting $x = \cos\theta$, the first three associated Legendre functions are

$$P_1^0(\cos\theta) = 1$$
$$P_1^0(\cos\theta) = \cos\theta$$
$$P_1^1(\cos\theta) = \sin\theta$$

and the orthogonality relation for them is

$$\int_0^\pi P_\ell^m(\cos\theta) P_{\ell'}^m(\cos\theta) \sin\theta d\theta = \frac{2}{2\ell+1}\frac{(\ell+m)!}{(\ell-m)!}\delta_{\ell\ell'}$$

The *Legendre polynomials*, P_ℓ, are generated by the Rodrigues formula,

$$P_\ell(x) = \frac{(-1)^\ell}{2^\ell \, \ell!} \frac{d^\ell}{dx^\ell}\left(1 - x^2\right)^\ell$$

The first three Legendre polynomials are

$$P_0(x) = 1$$
$$P_1(x) = x$$
$$P_2(x) = \frac{1}{2}\left(3x^2 - 1\right)$$

and the orthogonality relation for the Legendre polynomials is

$$\int_{-1}^{1} P_\ell(x) P_{\ell'}(x)\,dx = \frac{2}{2\ell + 1}\delta_{\ell\ell'}.$$

Solved Problem 6.3 Consider a particle with a wave function

$$\psi(x, y, z) = N[x + y + z]e^{-[(x^2 + y^2 + z^2)/\alpha^2]}$$

where N is a normalization constant and α is a parameter. We measure the values of L^2 and L_z. Find the probabilities that the measurements yield: (a) $L^2 = 2\hbar^2$ and $L_z = 0$, (b) $L^2 = 2\hbar^2$ and $L_z = \hbar$, and (c) $L^2 = 2\hbar^2$ and $L_z = -\hbar$. Use the known relations

$$Y_1^1(\theta, \varphi) = -\sqrt{\frac{3}{8\pi}}\sin\theta e^{i\varphi}$$

$$Y_1^0(\theta, \varphi) = \sqrt{\frac{3}{4\pi}}\cos\theta$$

$$Y_1^{-1}(\theta, \varphi) = \sqrt{\frac{3}{8\pi}}\sin\theta e^{-i\varphi}$$

Solution. First we must express the wave function in spherical coordinates.

$$\psi(r,\theta,\varphi) = Nr[\sin\theta(\cos\varphi + \sin\varphi] + \cos\theta]e^{-r^2/\alpha^2}$$

We can now separate variables so

$$\psi(r,\theta,\varphi) = R(r)T(\theta,\varphi)$$

where

$$R(r) = Nre^{-r^2/\alpha^2]}$$

and T can be expanded in spherical harmonics:

$$T(\theta,\varphi) = \sin\theta(\cos\varphi + \sin\varphi) + \cos\theta = \sum_{\ell,m} a_{\ell m} Y_\ell^m(\theta,\varphi)$$

We could use

$$a_{\ell m} = \langle \ell,m | T(\theta,\varphi) \rangle$$

to determine how much of each spherical harmonic is present, but in this case it may be simpler to do a little algebra:

$$T(\theta,\varphi) = \sin\theta\left(\frac{1}{2}\left(e^{i\varphi} + e^{-i\varphi}\right) + \frac{1}{2i}\left(e^{i\varphi} - e^{-i\varphi}\right)\right) + \sqrt{\frac{4\pi}{3}}Y_1^0$$

$$T(\theta,\varphi) = \frac{1}{2}\sin\theta\left(e^{i\varphi}(1-i) + e^{-i\varphi}(1+i)\right) + \sqrt{\frac{4\pi}{3}}Y_1^0$$

$$T(\theta,\varphi) = \frac{1}{2}\sqrt{\frac{8\pi}{3}}\left[-Y_1^1(1-i) + Y_1^{-1}(1+i)\right] + \sqrt{\frac{4\pi}{3}}Y_1^0$$

Now we should normalize T and then calculate the probability of each of the three states; however, in this case it may be simpler to calculate the relative probability of each of the three states, and then divide each relative probability by the sum of the relative probabilities.

$$P_{rel}(1,0) = \left|\sqrt{\frac{4\pi}{3}}\right|^2 = \frac{4\pi}{3}$$

$$P_{rel}(1,1) = \left| \frac{1}{2}\sqrt{\frac{8\pi}{3}}(i-1) \right|^2 = \frac{8\pi}{4 \cdot 3}(i-1)(-i-1) = \frac{2\pi}{3}(2) = \frac{4\pi}{3}$$

$$P_{rel}(1,-1) = \left| \frac{1}{2}\sqrt{\frac{8\pi}{3}}(1+i) \right|^2 = \frac{2\pi}{3}(1+i)(1-i) = \frac{2\pi}{3}(2) = \frac{4\pi}{3}$$

And since all three yield the same relative probability and these are the only three states present, we can say each will be measured with probability 1/3.

Spherically Symmetric Potentials

From classical mechanics we know that when a *spherically symmetric potential* $V(x, y, z) = V(r)$ acts on a particle, its angular momentum is a constant of the motion. In terms of quantum mechanics, this means that the angular momentum operator L^2 commutes with the hamiltonian

$$H = \frac{p^2}{2m} + V(r) = \frac{-\hbar^2}{2m}\frac{1}{r^2}\frac{\partial}{\partial r}\left(r^2\frac{\partial}{\partial r}\right) + \frac{L^2}{2mr^2} + V(r)$$

Since the angular dependence is found only in the L^2 term, we can separate variables in the wave function.

Solved Problem 6.4 Consider a particle in a spherical and infinite potential well

$$V(r) = \begin{cases} 0 & \text{for } 0 \le r \le a \\ \infty & \text{for } r > a \end{cases}$$

(a) Write the differential equations of the radial and angular parts, and solve the angular equation.

(b) Compute the energy levels and the stationary wave equation for $\ell = 0$.

Solution.

(a) We begin by writing the hamiltonian of the system:

$$H = \frac{p^2}{2m} + V(r) = \frac{-\hbar^2}{2m}\frac{1}{r^2}\frac{\partial}{\partial r}\left(r^2\frac{\partial}{\partial r}\right) + \frac{L^2}{2mr^2} + V(r)$$

For a stationary wave function we have

$$H\psi = \frac{-\hbar^2}{2m}\frac{1}{r^2}\frac{\partial}{\partial r}\left(r^2\frac{\partial}{\partial r}\psi\right) + \frac{L^2}{2mr^2}\psi + V(r)\psi = E\psi$$

Since H commutes with L^2, we can separate variables

$$\psi(r, \theta, \varphi) = R_{n\ell}(r)Y_\ell^m(\theta,\varphi)$$

The spherical harmonics are the angular solutions. Using the eigenvalue of L^2, we find the radial equation is

$$\frac{-\hbar^2}{2m}\frac{1}{r}\frac{\partial^2}{\partial r^2}\left(rR_{n\ell}(r)\right) + \left[\frac{\hbar^2\ell(\ell+1)}{2mr^2} + V(r)\right]R_{n\ell}(r) = ER_{n\ell}(r)$$

(b) For $\ell = 0$ we have

$$\frac{-\hbar^2}{2m}\frac{1}{r}\frac{\partial^2}{\partial r^2}\left(rR_{n0}(r)\right) + V(r)R_{n0}(r) = ER_{n0}(r)$$

We denote $R_{n0}(r) = R(r)$. For $r > a$ the potential is infinite and the wave function must vanish; therefore we have a boundary condition that $R(a) = 0$ and the derivative of $R(r)$ at $r = a$ will be discontinuous. For $0 \leq r \leq a$ we have:

$$\frac{-\hbar^2}{2m}\frac{1}{r}\frac{\partial^2}{\partial r^2}\left(rR(r)\right) = ER(r)$$

Change variables such that $U(r) = rR(r)$:

$$\frac{\partial^2 U(r)}{\partial r^2} + \frac{2mE}{\hbar^2}R(r) = 0$$

The solution is

$$U(r) = A\cos(kr) + B\sin(kr)$$

where

$$k = \sqrt{\frac{2mE}{\hbar^2}}$$

A and B are constants that can be determined using the boundary conditions; in addition to those mentioned above, one more can be deduced from $U(0) = rR(r)\big|_{r=0} = 0$. This condition gives $A = 0$ and the other states

$$U(a) = B\sin(ka) = 0$$

so that

$$ka = n\pi$$

This, with the definition of k, gives the energy eigenvalues

$$E_n = \frac{(n\pi\hbar)^2}{2ma^2}$$

Finally, to compute the value of B we use the normalization condition for the radial wave function

$$R(r) = \frac{U(r)}{r} = \begin{cases} B\dfrac{\sin(kr)}{r} & \text{for} \quad 0 \leq r \leq a \\ 0 & \text{for} \quad r > a \end{cases}$$

Hence,

$$\int_0^\infty |R(r)|^2 \, 4\pi r^2 dr = \int_0^a 4\pi B^2 \frac{\sin^2(kr)}{r^2} r^2 dr = \frac{2n\pi^2 B^2 a}{n\pi} = 1$$

and $B = (2\pi a)^{-1/2}$. Thus for $\ell = 0$ we have

$$\psi(r,\theta,\varphi) = R(r) = \frac{1}{\sqrt{2\pi a r}} \sin\left(\sqrt{\frac{2mE}{\hbar^2}}\, r\right)$$

Rotations

Let $|\psi\rangle$ be a state vector of a system in a certain coordinate system, O. To represent the state vector in another coordinate system, O', we define the *rotation operator*, U_R, such that

$$|\psi'\rangle = U_R|\psi\rangle$$

For a system O' obtained by the rotation of O around an axis in the direction of $\hat{n}$ with an angle θ, U_R is given as

$$U_R(\theta,\hat{n}) = e^{-i\theta\hat{n}\cdot L/\hbar}$$

where $\vec{L}$ is the angular momentum operator, which is said to be the *generator of rotation*. One can conclude from this definition that

$$\langle\psi'| = \langle\psi|U_R^\dagger$$

Note that to obtain U_R we usually use the infinitesimal rotation operator,

$$U_R(d\theta,\hat{n}) = 1 - \frac{i}{\hbar}\, d\theta\vec{L}\cdot\hat{n}$$

Remember

$$U_R(2\pi,\hat{n}) = U_R(0,\hat{n}) = 1$$

U_R can be used as a rotation operator not only for state vectors, but also for other operators or observables. Thus an observable, Q in the system O is transformed to Q' in the system O' such that

$$Q' = U_R Q U_R^\dagger$$
$$Q = U_R^\dagger Q' U_R$$

Solved Problem 6.5 Consider the infinitesimal rotation operator and find the rotation operator for a finite angle, θ. Hint: Define $d\theta = \theta/N$ for $N \to \infty$.

Solution. Using the conventions above,

$$|\psi'\rangle = [U_R(d\theta, \hat{n})]^N |\psi\rangle$$

Hence the rotation operator for a finite angle is

$$U_R(\theta, \hat{n}) = [U_R(d\theta, \hat{n})]^N$$

Using the given definition,

$$U_R(\theta, \hat{n}) = \lim_{N \to \infty} \left[1 - \frac{i}{\hbar} \vec{L} \cdot \hat{n} \frac{\theta}{N} \right]^N$$

Recall that

$$\lim_{N \to \infty} \left[1 + \frac{\alpha}{N} \right]^N = e^\alpha$$

Finally we obtain

$$U_R(\theta, \hat{n}) = \exp\left[\frac{-i}{\hbar} \theta \vec{L} \cdot \hat{n} \right]$$

Chapter 7
INTRINSIC ANGULAR MOMENTUM

Introduction

Spin is the common, if somewhat misleading, name of an intrinsic property of particles that was deduced from the Stern-Gerlach experiment. It is more properly called *intrinsic angular momentum*, so named because of the mathematical similarities between spin and (orbital) angular momentum. The formal definition of the spin operator is analogous to the orbital angular momentum operator:

$$S^2|s,m\rangle = s(s+1)\hbar^2|s,m\rangle$$
$$S_z|s,m\rangle = m\hbar|s,m\rangle$$

where $|s,m\rangle$ is an eigenfunction of S^2 and S_z. In any case where confusion might arise, we will instead label these states $|s,m_s\rangle$. The commutation relations for the spin operators are

$$\left[S_i, S_j \right] = i\hbar \sum_k \varepsilon_{ijk} S_k$$

$$\left[S_i, S^2 \right] = 0$$

Particles are classified as bosons if they have integer spin and fermions if they have half-integer spin. We will now concentrate on the most important group of fermions, those with spin 1/2, for example, the electron, the proton, and the neutron.

Spin One-Half

For spin 1/2, there are only two possible values of m, $\pm 1/2$, and we can label the eigenvectors $\left| \pm\frac{1}{2} \right\rangle$. In addition to the straightforward eigenvalue equations,

$$S^2 \left| \pm\frac{1}{2} \right\rangle = \frac{3}{4} \hbar^2 \left| \pm\frac{1}{2} \right\rangle$$

$$S_z \left| \pm\frac{1}{2} \right\rangle = \frac{\pm\hbar}{2} \left| \pm\frac{1}{2} \right\rangle$$

we can also define raising and lowering operators for spin and consider their action in this standard basis:

$$S_+ \left| \frac{1}{2} \right\rangle \equiv \left(S_x + iS_y \right) \left| \frac{1}{2} \right\rangle = 0$$

$$S_- \left| \frac{1}{2} \right\rangle \equiv \left(S_x - iS_y \right) \left| \frac{1}{2} \right\rangle = \hbar \left| \frac{-1}{2} \right\rangle$$

$$S_+ \left| \frac{-1}{2} \right\rangle = \hbar \left| \frac{1}{2} \right\rangle$$

$$S_- \left| \frac{-1}{2} \right\rangle = 0$$

As before, a raising operator either raises us to the next higher eigenstate or it returns zero if we're already in the highest eigenstate.

It is often convenient to use matrix representations of spin, where

$$\left|\frac{1}{2}\right\rangle = \begin{pmatrix} 1 \\ 0 \end{pmatrix}$$

$$\left|\frac{-1}{2}\right\rangle = \begin{pmatrix} 0 \\ 1 \end{pmatrix}$$

In this representation, the spin operators are proportional to the Pauli matrices, $\vec{S} = \dfrac{\hbar}{2}\vec{\sigma}$, where

$$\sigma_x = \begin{pmatrix} 0 & 1 \\ 1 & 0 \end{pmatrix}$$

$$\sigma_y = \begin{pmatrix} 0 & -i \\ i & 0 \end{pmatrix}$$

$$\sigma_z = \begin{pmatrix} 1 & 0 \\ 0 & -1 \end{pmatrix}$$

and $\sigma_x^2 = \sigma_y^2 = \sigma_z^2 = 1$.

⭐ Important!

Different texts represent the standard spin 1/2 basis vectors differently, and some books mix notation freely. Here are some of the common notations:

Spin up: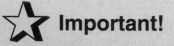

Spin down: $\left|\dfrac{-1}{2}\right\rangle = \begin{pmatrix} 0 \\ 1 \end{pmatrix} = |-\rangle = |\downarrow\rangle = \downarrow$

To relate the representation of a state $|\alpha\rangle$ in a given coordinate system O to the representation of the state $|\alpha'\rangle$ in a coordinate system O' that is rotated by an angle θ around an axis in the direction of the unit vector $\hat{u}$ we compute

$$|\alpha'\rangle = e^{-i\theta\hat{u}\cdot\vec{S}/\hbar}|\alpha\rangle$$

Thus the rotation matrix is

$$U_R = e^{-i\theta\hat{u}\cdot\vec{S}/\hbar} = \begin{pmatrix} \cos\left(\dfrac{\theta}{2}\right) & -\sin\left(\dfrac{\theta}{2}\right)e^{-i\varphi} \\ \sin\left(\dfrac{\theta}{2}\right)e^{i\varphi} & \cos\left(\dfrac{\theta}{2}\right) \end{pmatrix}$$

Notice that there is a factor of two difference between these angles and those in Chapter 6. The rotation of a *spin vector* is different from that of a spatial vector, and this can be used to define a spin vector, or *spinor*.

Solved Problem 7.1 Calculate $[\sigma_x, \sigma_y]$.

Solution.

$$[\sigma_x, \sigma_y] = \begin{pmatrix} 0 & 1 \\ 1 & 0 \end{pmatrix}\begin{pmatrix} 0 & -i \\ i & 0 \end{pmatrix} - \begin{pmatrix} 0 & -i \\ i & 0 \end{pmatrix}\begin{pmatrix} 0 & 1 \\ 1 & 0 \end{pmatrix}$$

$$[\sigma_x, \sigma_y] = \begin{pmatrix} i & 0 \\ 0 & -i \end{pmatrix} - \begin{pmatrix} -i & 0 \\ 0 & i \end{pmatrix} = 2i\begin{pmatrix} 1 & 0 \\ 0 & -1 \end{pmatrix} = 2i\sigma_z$$

Solved Problem 7.2 Using the matrix representations, calculate $S_i|\pm\rangle$.

Solution.

$$S_x|+\rangle = \frac{\hbar}{2}\begin{pmatrix} 0 & 1 \\ 1 & 0 \end{pmatrix}\begin{pmatrix} 1 \\ 0 \end{pmatrix} = \frac{\hbar}{2}\begin{pmatrix} 0 \\ 1 \end{pmatrix} = \frac{\hbar}{2}|-\rangle$$

$$S_x|-\rangle = \frac{\hbar}{2}\begin{pmatrix} 0 & 1 \\ 1 & 0 \end{pmatrix}\begin{pmatrix} 0 \\ 1 \end{pmatrix} = \frac{\hbar}{2}\begin{pmatrix} 1 \\ 0 \end{pmatrix} = \frac{\hbar}{2}|+\rangle$$

Notice that S_x produces a transition between the eigenstates of S_z, so that when S_x operates on one eigenstate, it produces a multiple of the other.

$$S_y|+\rangle = \frac{\hbar}{2}\begin{pmatrix} 0 & -i \\ i & 0 \end{pmatrix}\begin{pmatrix} 1 \\ 0 \end{pmatrix} = \frac{\hbar}{2}\begin{pmatrix} 0 \\ i \end{pmatrix} = \frac{i\hbar}{2}|-\rangle$$

$$S_y|-\rangle = \frac{\hbar}{2}\begin{pmatrix} 0 & -i \\ i & 0 \end{pmatrix}\begin{pmatrix} 0 \\ 1 \end{pmatrix} = \frac{\hbar}{2}\begin{pmatrix} -i \\ 0 \end{pmatrix} = \frac{-i\hbar}{2}|+\rangle$$

$$S_z|+\rangle = \frac{\hbar}{2}\begin{pmatrix} 1 & 0 \\ 0 & -1 \end{pmatrix}\begin{pmatrix} 1 \\ 0 \end{pmatrix} = \frac{\hbar}{2}\begin{pmatrix} 1 \\ 0 \end{pmatrix} = \frac{\hbar}{2}|+\rangle$$

$$S_z|-\rangle = \frac{\hbar}{2}\begin{pmatrix} 1 & 0 \\ 0 & -1 \end{pmatrix}\begin{pmatrix} 0 \\ 1 \end{pmatrix} = \frac{\hbar}{2}\begin{pmatrix} 0 \\ -1 \end{pmatrix} = \frac{-\hbar}{2}|-\rangle$$

These last two are eigenvalue equations, as expected.

Solved Problem 7.3 Consider a particle with spin 1/2. What are the eigenvalues and corresponding eigenvectors for S_x, S_y?

Solution. First find the eigenvalues of S_x:

$$\begin{vmatrix} -\lambda & \frac{\hbar}{2} \\ \frac{\hbar}{2} & -\lambda \end{vmatrix} = \lambda^2 - \left(\frac{\hbar}{2}\right)^2 = 0$$

So the eigenvalues are $\dfrac{\pm\hbar}{2}$, and we'll label the corresponding eigenvectors $|+\rangle_x, |-\rangle_x$. Solving for $|+\rangle_x$ we find

$$S_x|+\rangle_x = \frac{\hbar}{2}|+\rangle_x = \frac{\hbar}{2}\begin{pmatrix} a \\ b \end{pmatrix} = \frac{\hbar}{2}\begin{pmatrix} 0 & 1 \\ 1 & 0 \end{pmatrix}\begin{pmatrix} a \\ b \end{pmatrix} = \frac{\hbar}{2}\begin{pmatrix} b \\ a \end{pmatrix}$$

so that $a = b$. Normalization requires that $|a|^2 = |b|^2 = 1$, so

$$|+\rangle_x = \frac{1}{\sqrt{2}}\begin{pmatrix} 1 \\ 1 \end{pmatrix}$$

Similarly for the other eigenvector,

$$S_x|-\rangle_x = \frac{-\hbar}{2}|-\rangle_x = \frac{-\hbar}{2}\begin{pmatrix} c \\ d \end{pmatrix} = \frac{\hbar}{2}\begin{pmatrix} 0 & 1 \\ 1 & 0 \end{pmatrix}\begin{pmatrix} c \\ d \end{pmatrix} = \frac{\hbar}{2}\begin{pmatrix} d \\ c \end{pmatrix}$$

giving $c = -d$. After normalizing we find that

$$|-\rangle_x = \frac{1}{\sqrt{2}}\begin{pmatrix} 1 \\ -1 \end{pmatrix}$$

Following the same procedure for S_y,

$$\begin{vmatrix} -\lambda & \dfrac{-i\hbar}{2} \\[2mm] \dfrac{i\hbar}{2} & -\lambda \end{vmatrix} = \lambda^2 - \left(\frac{\hbar}{2}\right)^2 = 0$$

So the eigenvalues are $\dfrac{\pm\hbar}{2}$, and we'll label the corresponding eigenvectors $|+\rangle_y, |-\rangle_y$. Solving for $|+\rangle_y$ we find

$$S_y|+\rangle_y = \frac{\hbar}{2}|+\rangle_y = \frac{\hbar}{2}\begin{pmatrix} a \\ b \end{pmatrix} = \frac{\hbar}{2}\begin{pmatrix} 0 & -i \\ i & 0 \end{pmatrix}\begin{pmatrix} a \\ b \end{pmatrix} = \frac{\hbar}{2}\begin{pmatrix} -ib \\ ia \end{pmatrix}$$

so that $a = -ib$. Normalization requires that $|a|^2 + |b|^2 = 1$, so

$$|+\rangle_y = \frac{1}{\sqrt{2}}\begin{pmatrix} -i \\ 1 \end{pmatrix}$$

Similarly for the other eigenvector,

$$S_y|-\rangle_x = \frac{-\hbar}{2}|-\rangle_y = \frac{-\hbar}{2}\begin{pmatrix} c \\ d \end{pmatrix} = \frac{\hbar}{2}\begin{pmatrix} 0 & -i \\ i & 0 \end{pmatrix}\begin{pmatrix} c \\ d \end{pmatrix} = \frac{\hbar}{2}\begin{pmatrix} -id \\ ic \end{pmatrix}$$

giving $c = id$. After normalizing we find that

$$|-\rangle_y = \frac{1}{\sqrt{2}}\begin{pmatrix} 1 \\ i \end{pmatrix}$$

Solved Problem 7.4 Consider a particle in an eigenstate of S_x. If we measure the z-component of spin, what are the possible results and the probabilities of each?

Solution. The eigenvalues of S_z are $\dfrac{\pm\hbar}{2}$. The probability that we will measure $\dfrac{\hbar}{2}$ is

$$P\left(\frac{\hbar}{2}\right) = \left|_z\langle+|\pm\rangle_x\right|^2 = \frac{1}{2}$$

So whether the initial state is $|+\rangle_x$ or $|-\rangle_x$, there's a 50 percent chance of measuring the z-component of spin to be up.

Solved Problem 7.5 Find the result of applying the operators $S_x \pm iS_y$ on the eigenvectors $|\pm\rangle$ of S_z.

Solution. Begin with $S_x + iS_y$ and use the results of Solved Problem 7.2:

$$\left(S_x + iS_y\right)|+\rangle = S_x|+\rangle + iS_y|+\rangle = \frac{\hbar}{2}|-\rangle + i\frac{i\hbar}{2}|-\rangle = 0$$

$$\left(S_x + iS_y\right)|-\rangle = S_x|-\rangle + iS_y|-\rangle = \frac{\hbar}{2}|+\rangle + i\left(\frac{-i\hbar}{2}\right)|+\rangle = \hbar|+\rangle$$

So $S_x + iS_y$ is a spin-raising operator in that its action on spin down is to raise it to spin up. When applied to spin up, it has nowhere to raise it to, and so it returns zero.

$$\left(S_x - iS_y\right)|+\rangle = S_x|+\rangle - iS_y|+\rangle = \frac{\hbar}{2}|-\rangle - i\frac{i\hbar}{2}|-\rangle = \hbar|-\rangle$$

$$\left(S_x - iS_y\right)|-\rangle = S_x|-\rangle - iS_y|-\rangle = \frac{\hbar}{2}|+\rangle - i\left(\frac{-i\hbar}{2}\right)|+\rangle = 0$$

Similarly, $S_x - iS_y$ is a spin-lowering operator.

Interaction with a Magnetic Field

Consider a system consisting of particles with a spin $\vec{S}$. Applying a magnetic field $\vec{B}$ will introduce an additional term to the free hamiltonian, H_0, so that

$$H = H_0 + H_{\text{int}} = H_0 + \frac{e\vec{B}}{mc}\cdot\vec{S}$$

Notice that the dot product will be largest when the spin is aligned with the magnetic field.

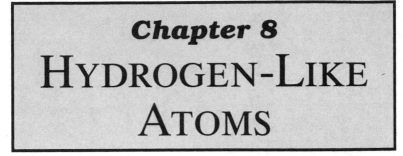

Chapter 8
HYDROGEN-LIKE ATOMS

IN THIS CHAPTER:

✔ *A Particle in a Central Potential*
✔ *Two Interacting Particles*
✔ *The Hydrogen Atom*
✔ *Hydrogen-Like Atoms*

A Particle in a Central Potential

The hamiltonian of a particle of mass M in a central potential is

$$H = \frac{p^2}{2M} + V(r) = \frac{-\hbar^2}{2M} \nabla^2 + V(r)$$

Part of the Laplacian in spherical coordinates can be written in terms of angular momentum, so this becomes

$$H = \frac{-\hbar^2}{2M} \frac{1}{r} \frac{\partial^2}{\partial r^2} + \frac{1}{2Mr^2} L^2 + V(r)$$

Since the components of $\vec{L}$ commute with L^2, they also commute with the hamiltonian, so there is a common basis for H, L^2, L_z.

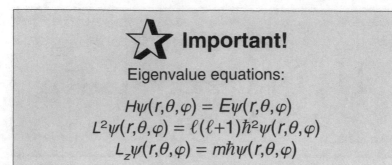

Using separation of variables, we can write

$$\psi(r,\theta,\varphi) = R_{n\ell}(r)Y_\ell^m(\theta,\varphi)$$

where the spherical harmonics involve the quantum numbers ℓ, m and the radial function involves the quantum numbers n, ℓ. Since the Y_ℓ^m are already normalized, the remaining normalization condition is

$$\int_0^\infty r^2 |R(r)|^2 dr = 1$$

Using the eigenvalue equation for L^2 in Schrödinger's equation, we arrive at the radial equation:

$$\left[\frac{-\hbar^2}{2M} \frac{1}{r} \frac{d^2}{dr^2} + \frac{\ell(\ell+1)\hbar^2}{2Mr^2} + V(r) \right] R_{n\ell}(r) = ER_{n\ell}(r)$$

We can simplify this equation using

$$R_{n\ell}(r) = \frac{1}{r} U_{n\ell}(r)$$

which gives

$$\left[\frac{-\hbar^2}{2M} \frac{d^2}{dr^2} + \left(\frac{\ell(\ell+1)\hbar^2}{2Mr^2} + V(r) \right) \right] U_{n\ell}(r) = EU_{n\ell}(r)$$

This now looks like a one-dimensional problem of a particle of mass M moving in an effective potential

$$V_{eff}(r) = V(r) + \frac{\ell(\ell+1)\hbar^2}{2Mr^2}$$

Solved Problem 8.1 Using the eigenvalue equations for a particle in a central potential, obtain the radial equation and the two angular equations.

Solution. Writing out the three eigenvalue equations:

$$\left\{ \frac{-\hbar^2}{2M}\left[\frac{1}{r}\frac{\partial^2}{\partial r^2} + \frac{1}{r^2}\left(\frac{\partial^2}{\partial\theta^2} + \cot\theta\frac{\partial}{\partial\theta} + \frac{1}{\sin^2\theta}\frac{\partial^2}{\partial\varphi^2}\right)\right] + V(r)\right\}\psi = E\psi$$

$$-\hbar^2\left(\frac{\partial^2}{\partial\theta^2} + \cot\theta\frac{\partial}{\partial\theta} + \frac{1}{\sin^2\theta}\frac{\partial^2}{\partial\varphi^2}\right)\psi = \ell(\ell+1)\hbar^2\psi$$

$$\left(-i\hbar\frac{\partial}{\partial\varphi}\right)\psi = m\hbar\psi$$

The second one can be used to eliminate the angular dependence from the first one:

$$\left\{ \frac{-\hbar^2}{2M}\left[\frac{1}{r}\frac{\partial^2}{\partial r^2} + \frac{1}{r^2}\left(-\ell(\ell+1)\right)\right] + V(r)\right\}\psi = E\psi$$

The separation of variables, $\psi(r,\theta,\varphi) = R_{n\ell}(r)Y_\ell^m(\theta,\varphi)$, allows us to write this as an equation in one variable:

$$\left\{ \frac{-\hbar^2}{2Mr}\frac{d^2}{dr^2} + \frac{\hbar^2\ell(\ell+1)}{2Mr^2} + V(r)\right\}R_{n\ell}(r) = ER_{n\ell}(r)$$

The equation for φ is particularly simple, so we can deduce that the φ-dependence of the spherical harmonics is

$$Y_\ell^m(\theta,\varphi) = e^{im\varphi}\Theta_\ell^m(\theta)$$

The remaining radial equation is

$$-\left(\frac{\partial^2}{\partial\theta^2} + \cot\theta \frac{\partial}{\partial\theta} + \frac{1}{\sin^2\theta}\frac{\partial^2}{\partial\varphi^2}\right) Y_\ell^m(\theta,\varphi) = \ell(\ell+1) Y_\ell^m(\theta,\varphi)$$

Two Interacting Particles

Consider a system of two spinless particles of mass m_1 and m_2 and positions $\vec{r}_1$ and $\vec{r}_2$. We assume the potential energy depends only on the distance between the particles, $V(\vec{r}_1 - \vec{r}_2)$. The study of the motion of the two particles is simplified if we adopt the coordinates of the *center of mass*,

$$\vec{r}_{cm} = \frac{m_1\vec{r}_1 + m_2\vec{r}_2}{m_1 + m_2}$$

and the *relative coordinate*,

$$\vec{r} = \vec{r}_1 - \vec{r}_2$$

We can then derive an equation for the center of mass motion

$$\frac{-\hbar^2}{2(m_1 + m_2)}\nabla^2\varphi(\vec{r}_{cm}) = E_{cm}\varphi(\vec{r}_{cm})$$

and an equation for the relative motion of the particles

$$\left[\frac{-\hbar^2}{2\mu}\nabla^2 + V(\vec{r})\right]\chi(\vec{r}) = E_r\chi(\vec{r})$$

where μ is the *reduced mass* of the two particles

$$\mu = \frac{m_1 m_2}{m_1 + m_2}$$

The first equation suggests that the center of mass behaves like a free particle of mass $m_1 + m_2$ and energy E_{cm}. The relative motion of the two particles is analogous to the motion of a particle of mass μ placed in a potential $V(\vec{r})$.

Solved Problem 8.2 Rather than viewing the hydrogen atom as an electron in a potential, let's consider it as two particles, an electron and a proton, with the *Coulomb potential* acting between them. This will allow us to find an equation for the motion of the center of mass and another for the relative motion of the electron and proton.

Solution. The Schrödinger equation for the proton (p) and electron (e) is

$$\left[\frac{-\hbar}{2}\left(\frac{\nabla_p^2}{m_p} + \frac{\nabla_e^2}{m_e} \right) + V(r) \right]\psi = E\psi$$

The potential between the particles is

$$V(r) = \frac{-e^2}{r} = \frac{-e^2}{\sqrt{x^2 + y^2 + z^2}} = \frac{-e^2}{\sqrt{\left(x_p - x_e\right)^2 + \left(y_p - y_e\right)^2 + \left(z_p - z_e\right)^2}}$$

For the differential operators we have

$$\frac{\partial^2}{\partial x_p^2} = \left(\frac{m_p}{m_p + m_e} \right)^2 \frac{\partial^2}{\partial x_{cm}^2} - \frac{2m_p}{m_p + m_e}\frac{\partial^2}{\partial x_{cm}\partial x} + \frac{\partial^2}{\partial x^2}$$

$$\frac{\partial^2}{\partial x_e^2} = \left(\frac{m_e}{m_p + m_e} \right)^2 \frac{\partial^2}{\partial x_{cm}^2} + \frac{2m_e}{m_p + m_e}\frac{\partial^2}{\partial x_{cm}\partial x} + \frac{\partial^2}{\partial x^2}$$

and similarly for y,z. Substituting these operators in gives

$$\frac{-\hbar^2}{2}\left\{ \left[\frac{1}{m_p + m_e}\left(\nabla_{cm}^2\right) + \frac{1}{\mu}\left(\nabla^2\right) \right] - \frac{e^2}{r} \right\}\psi = E\psi$$

We separate the wave function into two parts, one that depends only on the center of mass coordinates and one that depends only on the relative coordinates, $\psi(r_{cm}, r) = \varphi(r_{cm})\chi(r)$.

$$\frac{-\hbar^2}{2\varphi(r_{cm})}\left[\frac{1}{m_p + m_e}\nabla^2_{cm}\varphi(r_{cm})\right] = \frac{\hbar^2}{2\chi(r)}\left[\frac{1}{\mu}\nabla^2 + \frac{e^2}{r}\right]\chi(r) + E$$

Each side must be independently equal to a constant, so the center of mass motion is described by

$$\frac{-\hbar^2}{2\varphi(r_{cm})}\left[\frac{1}{m_p + m_e}\nabla^2_{cm}\varphi(r_{cm})\right] = E_{cm}$$

where E_{cm} is translational kinetic energy, and the relative motion is described by

$$\frac{\hbar^2}{2\chi(r)}\left[\frac{1}{\mu}\nabla^2 + \frac{e^2}{r}\right]\chi(r) + E_r = 0$$

To obtain the wave function of the hydrogen atom's electron, it is this latter equation we must solve.

The Hydrogen Atom

The hydrogen atom consists of an electron and proton bound by electrostatics, and their potential energy is

$$V(r) = \frac{-e^2}{r}$$

where r is the distance between the two particles. Since the mass of the proton is much greater than the mass of the electron, the reduced mass of the system is very close to the electron mass and the center of mass is almost exactly where the proton is. To good approximation we can consider the proton at the center of mass and all we need do is solve for the electron's position relative to the proton. It will be convenient to use the *Bohr radius*,

$$a_0 = \frac{\hbar^2}{\mu e^2} \cong 0.052 \text{ nm}$$

and the *ionization energy* of the hydrogen atom

$$E_1 = \frac{\mu e^4}{2\hbar^2} \cong 13.6 \text{ eV}$$

Earlier we found that we can write the states of the system as

$$\psi_{n\ell m}(r,\theta,\varphi) = \frac{1}{r}U_{n\ell}(r)Y_\ell^m(\theta,\varphi)$$

To solve the radial wave equation, we define $\rho = \dfrac{r}{a_0}$ and $\lambda_{k\ell} = \sqrt{\dfrac{-E_{k\ell}}{E_1}}$ and write

$$\left[\frac{d^2}{d\rho^2} - \frac{\ell(\ell+1)}{\rho^2} + \frac{2}{\rho} - \lambda_{k\ell}^2\right]U_{k\ell}(\rho) = 0$$

where $n = k + \ell$. As ρ approaches infinity, the constant term dominates, and we expect a dying (real) exponential. For small ρ the centrifugal term dominates, and we expect powers of ρ. Using these limits and the ever-popular series expansion, we write the function as

$$U_{k\ell}(\rho) = \left(e^{-\rho\lambda_{k\ell}}\right)\left(\rho^s\right)\left(\sum_{q=0}^{\infty} C_q\rho^q\right)$$

The coefficients can be obtained from the recursion relation

$$C_q = \left(\frac{-2}{k+1}\right)^q \frac{(k-1)!}{(k-q-1)!}\frac{(2\ell+1)!}{(q+2\ell+1)!}C_0$$

once C_0 is determined through normalization. The solution is then

$$R_{n\ell}(\rho) = -\sqrt{\left(\frac{2}{na_0}\right)^3 \frac{(n-\ell-1)!}{2n\left[(n+1)!\right]^3}}\, e^{-\rho/2}\rho^{\ell} L_{n+1}^{2\ell+1}(\rho)$$

where the associated Laguerre polynomials are

$$L_l^m(x) = \frac{d^m}{dx^m} L_l(x) = \frac{d^m}{dx^m}\left[e^x \frac{d^l}{dx^l}\left(x^l e^{-x}\right)\right]$$

For fixed ℓ there exist an infinite number of possible energy values:

$$E_{k\ell} = \frac{-E_n}{(k+\ell)^2}$$

Each of them is at least $(2\ell + 1)$-fold degenerate. This essential degeneracy results from the radial equation being independent of the quantum number m. Some of the energy values manifest accidental degeneracy. Here the $E_{k\ell}$ do not depend on k and ℓ separately, but only on their sum. We set $n = k + \ell$ and then

$$E_n = \frac{-E_1}{n^2} = \frac{-13.6 \text{ eV}}{n^2}$$

The shell characterized by n is said to contain n subshells, each corresponding to one of the values of ℓ:

$$\ell = 0,1,2,...,n-1$$

Each subshell contains $2\ell + 1$ distinct states corresponding to the possible values of m:

$$m = -\ell, -\ell+1,...,\ell-1,\ell$$

The total degeneracy of the energy level E_n is

$$g_n = \sum_{\ell=0}^{n-1} (2\ell+1) = n^2$$

If one takes into account the electron's spin, then this number of degenerate states should be multiplied by two.

For historical reasons (from the period in which the study of atomic spectra resulted in empirical classification of the lines observed) the various values ℓ of are associated with letters of the alphabet as follows:

$$\ell = 0 \leftrightarrow s$$
$$\ell = 1 \leftrightarrow p$$
$$\ell = 2 \leftrightarrow d$$
$$\ell = 3 \leftrightarrow f$$
$$\ell = 4 \leftrightarrow g$$

and continuing in alphabetical order thereafter.

Hydrogen-Like Atoms

The results obtained above originate in calculations for systems of two particles with mutual attraction potential inversely proportional to the distance between them. There are many physical systems that satisfy this condition, at least approximately: deuterium, tritium, ions that contain only one electron, muonic atoms, positronium, etc. The results are applicable to these systems, provided that we properly select the constants introduced in the calculations. For example, if the charge of the nucleus is Ze, then $e^2 \rightarrow Ze^2$ in all the calculations.

Solved Problem 8.3 The wave function of an electron in a hydrogen-like atom is $\psi(r) = Ce^{-r/a}$ where $a = a_0/Z$. The nuclear charge is Ze and the atom contains only one electron.

(a) Compute the normalization constant.

(b) If the nuclear numbers are $A = 173$ and $Z = 70$, what is the probability that the electron is in the nucleus? Assume that the radius of the nucleus is $1.2 \times A^{1/3}$ fm.

(c) What is the probability that the electron is in the region $x,y,z > 0$?

Solution.

(a) For normalization, $\iiint \psi^* \psi d^3 r = 1$ which implies

$$|C|^2 \int_0^\infty r^2 e^{-2r/a} dr \int_0^{2\pi} d\varphi \int_0^\pi \sin\theta d\theta = 4\pi |C|^2 \int_0^\infty r^2 e^{-2r/a} dr = 1$$

$$\int_0^\infty r^2 e^{-2r/a} dr = \left(\frac{a}{2}\right)^3 \Gamma(3) = \left(\frac{a}{2}\right)^3 2! = \frac{a^3}{4}$$

Therefore, $C = (\pi a^3)^{-1/2}$.

(b) Let R be the radius of the nucleus. The probability that the electron will be found in the nucleus is

$$P = \int_0^R r^2 |\psi(r)|^2 dr (4\pi) = 4\pi C^2 \int_0^R r^2 e^{-r/a} dr$$

Since R is small compared to a, we can consider the wave function constant, in particular $e^{-2R/a} \cong 1$, so

$$P = \frac{4}{3}\left(\frac{R}{a}\right)^3 = \frac{4}{3}\left(\frac{Zr_0}{a_0}\right)^3 A = 1.1 \times 10^{-6}$$

(c) The wave function is independent of both angles, so the probability that the electron is found in 1/8 of the space is simply 1/8.

Chapter 9
PARTICLE MOTION IN AN ELECTROMAGNETIC FIELD

IN THIS CHAPTER:

- ✔ *Electromagnetic Fields and Potentials*
- ✔ *The Hamiltonian*
- ✔ *The Magnetic Moment*

Electromagnetic Fields and Potentials

Consider an electromagnetic field characterized by the values of the electric field, $\vec{E}(\vec{r},t)$, and of the magnetic field, $\vec{B}(\vec{r},t)$. These fields are not independent since they must satisfy Maxwell's equations. Because of this interrelationship, it is possible to introduce a *scalar potential*, $\varphi(\vec{r},t)$, and a *vector potential*, $\vec{A}(\vec{r},t)$, such that

$$\vec{E} = -\vec{\nabla}\varphi - \frac{1}{c}\frac{\partial \vec{A}}{\partial t}$$

$$\vec{B} = \vec{\nabla} \times \vec{A}$$

When $\vec{E}$ and $\vec{B}$ are given, φ and $\vec{A}$ are not uniquely determined. When we choose a particular set of potentials, we say we choose a *gauge*. From one set of potentials $(\varphi, \vec{A})$ we can obtain another set $(\varphi', \vec{A}')$ by performing a *gauge transformation*:

$$\varphi' = \varphi - \frac{1}{c}\frac{\partial f(\vec{r},t)}{\partial t}$$

$$\vec{A}' = \vec{A} + \vec{\nabla}f(\vec{r},t)$$

where $f(\vec{r},t)$ is an arbitrary function. The equations describing the physical system involve the potentials, but we shall see that in quantum mechanics, as in classical physics, the predictions of the theory do not depend on the gauge chosen. This important property is called *gauge invariance*.

As an example, consider two gauges describing a constant magnetic field in the z direction. The symmetric gauge where $\vec{A} \equiv \frac{1}{2}\vec{r} \times \vec{B} = \frac{B_0}{2}(-y, x, 0)$ gives $\vec{B} = \vec{\nabla} \times \vec{A} = B_0\hat{z}$. And in the Landau gauge we have $\vec{A} = (-B_0 y, 0, 0)$, which also gives $B_0\hat{z}$.

Solved Problem 9.1 Consider the example above of two gauges describing a constant magnetic field $\vec{B} = B_0\hat{z}$. Determine the gauge function $f(\vec{r},t)$ relating the two gauges.

Solution. Define

$$\vec{A} = \frac{B_0}{2}(-y, x, 0)$$

$$\vec{A}' = B_0(-y, 0, 0)$$

and consider the components of the gauge-transformed vector potential

$$A_x' = -B_0 y = A_x + \partial_x f = \frac{-B_0 y}{2} + \partial_x f$$

$$A_y' = 0 = A_y + \partial_y f = \frac{B_0 x}{2} + \partial_y f$$

From this we can conclude that

$$\frac{\partial f}{\partial x} = \frac{-B_0 y}{2}$$

$$\frac{\partial f}{\partial y} = \frac{-B_0 x}{2}$$

Integration gives

$$f(x, y) = \frac{-B_0}{2} xy + \text{constant}$$

The Hamiltonian

Consider a particle of mass m and charge q. The classical equation of motion in the presence of electric and magnetic fields $\vec{E}, \vec{B}$ is

$$m\frac{d^2\vec{r}}{dt^2} = q\vec{E} + \frac{q}{c}\vec{v} \times \vec{B}$$

The hamiltonian that leads to this equation of motion is

$$H = \frac{1}{2m}\left(\vec{p} - \frac{q}{c}\vec{A}\right) \cdot \left(\vec{p} - \frac{q}{c}\vec{A}\right) + q\varphi$$

In this chapter we use a semi-classical theory for particle motion in an electromagnetic field. In this theory, the field is analogous to a classical field, while the system is treated according to the postulates of quantum mechanics. Thus the particle is described by a wave function and the hamiltonian is written as above, but now $\vec{p}, \vec{A}, \varphi$ represent the corresponding operators.

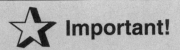

Important!

When we perform a gauge transformation in this semiclassical quantum theory, we must also transform the wave function as

$$\Psi'(\vec{r},t) = e^{iqf(\vec{r},t)/c\hbar}\,\Psi(\vec{r},t)$$

in addition to transforming the potentials as before

$$\varphi' = \varphi - \frac{1}{c}\frac{\partial f(\vec{r},t)}{\partial t}$$

$$\vec{A}' = \vec{A} + \vec{\nabla}f(\vec{r},t)$$

Given a wave function $\Psi(\vec{r},t)$, the probability density is

$$\rho = |\Psi(\vec{r}_0,t)|^2$$

where ρ expresses the probability of finding the particle at time t at the point $\vec{r}_0$. For particles with mass m and charge q, the probability current density is

$$\vec{s} = \frac{1}{2m}\left[\frac{\hbar}{i}\left(\Psi^*\vec{\nabla}\Psi - \Psi\vec{\nabla}\Psi^*\right) - \frac{2q}{c}\vec{A}\Psi^*\Psi\right]$$

Both ρ and $\vec{s}$ do not depend on the gauge chosen, and they are said to be gauge invariant.

Solved Problem 9.2 According to the postulates of quantum mechanics, a given physical system is characterized by a state vector $|\Psi\rangle$. Consider a particle of mass m and charge q influenced by an electric field $\vec{E}$ and a magnetic field $\vec{B}$.

(a) Write the hamiltonian with $\vec{A}, \varphi$ and then with $\vec{A}', \varphi'$.

(b) Write the Schrödinger equation for each case.

(c) Show that if Ψ is the solution of the first equation then

$$\Psi'(\vec{r},t) = e^{\frac{iqf(\vec{r},t)}{c\hbar}} \Psi(\vec{r},t)$$

is the solution of the second one.

(d) Discuss the results. How does the state vector depend on the choice of gauge?

Solution.

(a) Using gauge invariance, the two hamiltonians are

$$H = \frac{1}{2m}\left(\vec{p} - \frac{q}{c}\vec{A}\right) \cdot \left(\vec{p} - \frac{q}{c}\vec{A}\right) + q\varphi$$

$$H' = \frac{1}{2m}\left(\vec{p} - \frac{q}{c}\vec{A}'\right) \cdot \left(\vec{p} - \frac{q}{c}\vec{A}'\right) + q\varphi'$$

$$H' = \frac{1}{2m}\left(\vec{p} - \frac{q}{c}\vec{A} - \frac{q}{c}\vec{\nabla}f\right) \cdot \left(\vec{p} - \frac{q}{c}\vec{A} - \frac{q}{c}\vec{\nabla}f\right) + q\varphi - \frac{q}{c}\frac{\partial f}{\partial t}$$

(b) The first Schrödinger equation is

$$\left[\frac{1}{2m}\left(\frac{\hbar}{i}\vec{\nabla} - \frac{q}{c}\vec{A}\right)^2 + q\varphi\right]\Psi(\vec{r},t) = i\hbar\frac{\partial\Psi(\vec{r},t)}{\partial t}$$

For the second, we also put in the momentum operator:

$$\left[\frac{1}{2m}\left(\frac{\hbar}{i}\vec{\nabla} - \frac{q}{c}\vec{A} - \frac{q}{c}\vec{\nabla}f\right)^2 + q\varphi - \frac{q}{c}\frac{\partial f}{\partial t}\right]\Psi'(\vec{r},t) = i\hbar\frac{\partial\Psi'(\vec{r},t)}{\partial t}$$

(c) Show that $\Psi' = e^{\frac{iqf}{c\hbar}}\Psi$ is a solution of the second equation.

$$i\hbar \frac{\partial}{\partial t}\left[e^{\frac{iqf}{c\hbar}}\Psi \right] = i\hbar\left[\frac{iq}{c\hbar}\left(\frac{\partial f}{\partial t} \right)e^{\frac{iqf}{c\hbar}}\Psi + e^{\frac{iqf}{c\hbar}}\frac{\partial \Psi}{\partial t} \right]$$

$$i\hbar \frac{\partial \Psi'}{\partial t} = \left[\frac{-q}{c}\left(\frac{\partial f}{\partial t} \right)\Psi' + e^{\frac{iqf}{c\hbar}}\left\{ \left[\frac{1}{2m}\left(\frac{\hbar}{i}\vec{\nabla} - \frac{q}{c}\vec{A} \right)^2 + q\varphi \right]e^{\frac{-iqf}{c\hbar}}\Psi' \right\} \right]$$

$$i\hbar \frac{\partial \Psi'}{\partial t} = \left[\left\{ \frac{-q}{c}\left(\frac{\partial f}{\partial t} \right) + q\varphi \right\}\Psi' + e^{\frac{iqf}{c\hbar}}\frac{1}{2m}\left(\frac{\hbar}{i}\vec{\nabla} - \frac{q}{c}\vec{A} \right)^2 e^{\frac{-iqf}{c\hbar}}\Psi' \right]$$

Let's concentrate on that last problem term:

$$e^{\frac{iqf}{c\hbar}}\left(\frac{\hbar}{i}\vec{\nabla} - \frac{q}{c}\vec{A} \right)^2 e^{\frac{-iqf}{c\hbar}}\Psi' = \left(\frac{\hbar}{i}\left[\vec{\nabla} + \frac{-iq}{c\hbar}\vec{\nabla}f \right] - \frac{q}{c}\vec{A} \right)^2 \Psi'$$

The extra term appears when we move the exponential back through the gradient operator, which must act on the gauge function in the exponential. Plugging this back in gives the requested result.

(d) We see that when we pass from one gauge to another, the state vector describing the system is transformed by a unitary transformation involving the gauge function. For the wave function, the gauge transformation corresponds to a phase change that varies from one point to another and is therefore not a global phase factor. However, the physical predictions obtained by using the wave functions are the same since the operators that describe physical quantities are also transformed when we change between the gauges.

The Magnetic Moment

For a particle with a magnetic moment $\vec{\mu}_s$ in a magnetic field $\vec{B}$, the interaction hamiltonian is

$$H_{\text{int}} = -\vec{\mu}_s \cdot \vec{B}$$

This term should be added to the hamiltonian developed earlier for a charge in an electromagnetic field. An electron of spin $\vec{S}$ has a magnetic moment

$$\vec{\mu} = \frac{-eg}{2mc}\vec{S}$$

where g is the gyromagnetic ratio.

★ Note!

The gyromagnetic ratio is very close to 2:

$$g = 2\left(1 + \frac{\alpha}{2\pi} + \cdots\right) = 2.002331836$$

This calculated value can be compared to the measured value, 2.002331841, demonstrating remarkable agreement between theory and experiment.

Solved Problem 9.3 In this problem we examine how the energy levels of the hydrogen atom are modified in the presence of a static magnetic field; this effect is called the *Zeeman effect* (we'll ignore the normal Zeeman effect, which is related to spin). Suppose the mass of the electron is m and its charge is q.

(a) We denote by H_0 the hamiltonian of the electron in the hydrogen atom without a magnetic field. Write the eigenstates of H_0 that are also eigenstates of L^2, L_z. What are the corresponding eigenvalues?

(b) Suppose that the atom is placed in a uniform magnetic field B_0 along the z axis. The new hamiltonian will be

$$H_0 + H_1 = H_0 + \frac{qB}{8m}\left(x^2 + y^2\right) - \frac{\mu_B}{\hbar}B_0 L_z$$

Are the states of part (a) also eigenstates of the new hamiltonian? How are the energy levels modified? Assume that the term $\frac{qB}{8m}\left(x^2 + y^2\right)$ is negligible compared to $\frac{\mu_B}{\hbar}B_0 L_z$ (this can be shown by a detailed calculation).

Solution.

(a) The eigenstates of the hamiltonian of the hydrogen atom are

$$\psi_{n\ell m}(r, \theta, \varphi) = R_{n\ell}(r)Y_{\ell}^{m}(\theta, \varphi)$$

The number n determines the energy level, $E_n = \dfrac{-E_1}{n^2}$. The energy levels in a hydrogen atom are degenerate; for each n, the number ℓ can assume the values $\ell = 0,1,2, \ldots, n-1$ and m is an integer between $-\ell$ and ℓ. The total degeneracy (without spin) is n^2. The wave function given above is an eigenfunction L^2 of with eigenvalue $\ell(\ell+1)\hbar^2$ and of L_z with eigenvalue $m\hbar$.

(b) Neglecting the term we're told is small, we have

$$H = H_0 - \frac{\mu_B}{\hbar} B_0 L_z$$

Since the wave function is an eigenfunction of both H_0 and L_z, it will also be an eigenfunction of H; however, the new term will alter the energy eigenvalues, and since this new addition to the energies depends on m, it will break the degeneracy:

$$\left[H_0 - \frac{\mu_B}{\hbar} B_0 L_z \right] \psi_{n\ell m} = \left(E_n - m\mu B_0 \right) \psi_{n\ell m}$$

Chapter 10
PERTURBATION THEORY

Time-Independent Perturbation Theory

The quantum mechanical study of a *conservative system* (whose hamiltonian is not explicitly time dependent) is based on the eigenvalue equation of the hamiltonian operator. Some systems, for example, the harmonic oscillator, are simple enough to be solved exactly. In general, the equation is not amenable to analytic solutions and an approximate solution is sought.

In this section, we present the widely used time-independent perturbation theory. This method is encountered often throughout physics. We begin by studying the primary factors that produce the main properties of the system, then we attempt to explain the secondary effects neglected in the first approximation.

Perturbation theory is appropriate when the hamiltonian of the system can be put in the form

$$H = H_0 + \lambda W$$

where the eigenstates and eigenvalues of H_0 are known and λ is a parameter. The operator λW must be much smaller than H_0, that is,

$$\lambda W \ll H_0$$

For example, $\lambda \ll 1$ if the matrix elements of W are comparable to those of H_0.

We assume that the unperturbed energies (that is, the eigenvalues of H_0) form a discrete spectrum, E_p^0, where p is an integral index. We denote the corresponding eigenstates by $|\varphi_p^i\rangle$ where the index i distinguishes among the different linearly independent eigenvectors corresponding to the same eigenvalue in the case of a degenerate eigenvalue. We have

$$H_0|\varphi_p^i\rangle = E_p^0|\varphi_p^i\rangle$$

where $|\varphi_p^i\rangle$ form an orthonormal basis of the state space.

When the parameter λ is equal to zero, the hamiltonian is unperturbed. The eigenvalues $E(\lambda)$ of $H(\lambda)$ generally depend on λ. In the case of a nondegenerate energy level, the perturbation may either affect the energy level or not affect it. For a degenerate energy level, it is possible that the perturbation splits the level into distinct energy levels, removing the degeneracy. The perturbation may also leave a degeneracy remaining.

We are looking for the eigenstates, $|\psi(\lambda)\rangle$ and eigenvalues $E(\lambda)$ of the hamiltonian $H(\lambda)$:

$$H(\lambda)|\psi(\lambda)\rangle = E(\lambda)|\psi(\lambda)\rangle$$

We shall assume that $E(\lambda)$ and $|\psi(\lambda)\rangle$ can be expanded in power series of λ in the form

$$E(\lambda) = \varepsilon_0 + \lambda\varepsilon_1 + \cdots + \lambda^q\varepsilon_q$$

$$|\psi(\lambda)\rangle = |0\rangle + \lambda|1\rangle + \cdots + \lambda^q|q\rangle$$

When $\lambda \ll 1$, each element in a series expansion is much smaller than the previous one, and it usually suffices to consider only the first few elements. The element containing λ is called the first-order correction, the one containing λ^2 is called the second-order correction, etc.

Solved Problem 10.1 Consider a particular nondegenerate eigenvalue, E_n^0, of the unperturbed hamiltonian, with eigenvector $|\varphi_n\rangle$. Derive first- and second-order corrections for the energy level and corresponding eigenvector.

Solution. Substituting the series expansions into the Schrödinger equation, we obtain

$$\left(H_0 + \lambda W\right)\left[\sum_{q=0}^{\infty} \lambda^q |q\rangle\right] = \left[\sum_{q'=0}^{\infty} \lambda^{q'} \varepsilon_{q'}\right]\left[\sum_{q=0}^{\infty} \lambda^q |q\rangle\right]$$

By equating the coefficients of successive powers of λ we find

$$H_0|0\rangle = \varepsilon_0|0\rangle$$

$$(H_0 - \varepsilon_0)|1\rangle + (W - \varepsilon_1)|0\rangle = 0$$

$$(H_0 - \varepsilon_0)|2\rangle + (W - \varepsilon_1)|1\rangle - \varepsilon_2|0\rangle = 0$$

The first of these tells us that $|\varphi_n\rangle \propto |0\rangle$ and we'll choose them to be equal. We can choose the normalization and phase,

$$\langle 0|0\rangle = 1$$

$$\langle 0|1\rangle = \langle 1|0\rangle = 0$$

$$\langle 0|2\rangle = \langle 2|0\rangle = \frac{-1}{2}\langle 1|1\rangle$$

and can conclude that

$$\langle \varphi_n|(H_0 - \varepsilon_0)|1\rangle + \langle \varphi_n|(W - \varepsilon_1)|0\rangle = 0$$

$$\varepsilon_1 = \langle \varphi_n|W|0\rangle = \langle \varphi_n|W|\varphi_n\rangle$$

You Need To Know ✔

To first order we have

$$E_n(\lambda) = E_n^{(0)} + \lambda \langle \varphi_n | W | \varphi_n \rangle$$

$$|\psi_n(\lambda)\rangle = |\varphi_n\rangle + \lambda \sum_{p \neq n} \frac{\langle \varphi_p | W | \varphi_n \rangle}{E_n^{(0)} - E_p^{(0)}} |\varphi_p\rangle$$

in other words, the first-order correction to the energy is the mean value of the perturbation term in the unperturbed state. To second order the energy is

$$E_n(\lambda) = E_n^{(0)} + \lambda \langle \varphi_n | W | \varphi_n \rangle + \lambda^2 \sum_{p \neq n} \frac{\left| \langle \varphi_p | W | \varphi_n \rangle \right|^2}{E_n^{(0)} - E_p^{(0)}}$$

Perturbation of a Degenerate State

Assume that the level E_n^0 is g_n-fold degenerate. We present a method for calculating the first-order correction for the energies and the zero-order correction for the eigenstates.

Arrange the numbers $\langle \varphi_n^i | W | \varphi_n^{i'} \rangle$ in a $g_n \times g_n$ matrix, which we denote $W^{(n)}$ and which we recognize as a chunk of the matrix that represents W in the $\{|\varphi_p^i\rangle\}$ basis. Note that $W^{(n)}$ is not identical to W; it is an operator in the g_n-dimensional space corresponding to the energy level E_n^0.

The first-order corrections ε_1^j of the energy level E_n^0 are eigenvalues of the matrix $W^{(n)}$. The zero-order eigenstates corresponding to E_n^0 are the eigenvectors of $W^{(n)}$. Let ε_1^j ($j = 1,2,...,f_n^{(1)}$) be the roots of the characteristic equation of $W^{(n)}$ (that is, its eigenvalues), then the degenerate energy level splits, to the first order, into $f_n^{(1)}$ distinct sublevels:

$$E_{n,k}(\lambda) = E_n^{(0)} + \lambda \varepsilon_1^j$$

When $f_n^{(1)} = g_n$ we say that to first order the perturbation W completely removes the degeneracy of the level E_n^0. When $f_n^{(1)} < g_n$ the degeneracy is only partially removed, or not at all if $f_n^{(1)} = 1$.

Suppose that a specific sublevel

$$E_{n,k}(\lambda) = E_n^{(0)} + \lambda \varepsilon_1^j$$

is q-fold degenerate, in the sense that there are q linearly independent eigenvectors of $W^{(n)}$ corresponding to it. We distinguish between two completely different situations:

1. Suppose there is only one exact energy level $E(\lambda)$ that is equal to the first order to $E_{n,j}$. This energy is q-fold degenerate. In this case the zero-order eigenvector $|0\rangle$ of $H(\lambda)$ cannot be completely specified, since the only condition is that this vector belongs to the q-dimensional eigensubspace of $H(\lambda)$ corresponding to $E(\lambda)$. This situation often arises when the H_0 and λW possess common symmetry properties, implying an essential degeneracy of $H(\lambda)$.

2. A second possibility arises when several different energies $E(\lambda)$ are equal to first order to $E_{n,j}$. The difference between these energies appears in calculation of the second or higher orders. In this case an eigenvector of $H(\lambda)$ corresponding to one of these energies certainly approaches an eigenvector of $E_{n,j}$ for $\lambda \to 0$; the inverse, however, does not hold.

Solved Problem 10.2 Consider a hydrogen atom placed in a uniform static electric field ε that points in the z direction. The term that corresponds to this interaction in the hamiltonian is

$$W = -e\varepsilon z$$

Note that for the electric fields typically produced in a laboratory, the condition $W \ll H_0$ is satisfied. The appearance of the perturbation removes the degeneracy from some of the hydrogen states. This phenomenon is called the *Stark effect*. Calculate the Stark effect for $n = 2$ in a hydrogen atom.

Solution. Before we explicitly calculate the matrix elements of the perturbation, we note that the perturbation has nonzero matrix elements only between states of opposite parity; as we are considering the $n = 2$ level, the relevant states are those with $\ell = 0$ and $\ell = 1$. Using symmetry, the m-values of the two states must be equal. Therefore there are only two non-zero matrix elements:

$$
W_s = \begin{pmatrix}
0 & \langle 2s|W|2p,0\rangle & 0 & 0 \\
\langle 2p,0|W|2s\rangle & 0 & 0 & 0 \\
0 & 0 & 0 & 0 \\
0 & 0 & 0 & 0
\end{pmatrix}
$$

An explicit calculation gives $\langle 2p,0|W|2s\rangle = 3ea_0\varepsilon$ where a_0 is the Bohr radius. Note that the matrix element is linear in ε, so this correction is called the *linear Stark effect*. We transform to the basis that diagonalizes the perturbation; this basis is

$$
\left\{ |2p,-1\rangle, |2p,1\rangle, \frac{1}{\sqrt{2}}\big(|2s,0\rangle+|2p,0\rangle\big), \frac{1}{\sqrt{2}}\big(|2s,0\rangle-|2p,0\rangle\big) \right\}
$$

Time-Dependent Perturbation Theory

Consider a physical system with the hamiltonian H_0. We assume the spectrum of H_0 to be discrete and nondegenerate (the formulas can be generalized to other situations). We have

$$
H_0|\varphi_n\rangle = E_n|\varphi_n\rangle
$$

Suppose that H_0 is time-independent but that at $t = 0$ a time-dependent perturbation is applied to the system

$$
H(t) = H_0 + \lambda W(t)
$$

Where λ is a parameter, $\lambda \ll 1$, and $W(t)$ is an operator of the same magnitude as H_0. Suppose the system is initially in the state $|\varphi_i\rangle$, which is an eigenstate of H_0 with eigenvalue E_i. We present an expression for calculating the first-order approximation of the probability $P_{if}(t)$ of finding the system in another eigenstate $|\varphi_f\rangle$ of H_0 at time t:

$$P_{if}(t) = \frac{\lambda^2}{\hbar^2}\left|\int_0^t e^{i\omega_{if}t'} W_{if}(t')\,dt'\right|^2$$

where ω_{if} is the *Bohr angular frequency* defined by

$$\omega_{if} = \frac{E_i - E_f}{\hbar}$$

and $W_{if}(t)$ is the matrix element of $W(t)$:

$$W_{fi}(t) = \langle \varphi_f | W(t) | \varphi_i \rangle$$

Consider now the case of transition between a state $|\varphi_i\rangle$ and a state $|\varphi_f\rangle$ of energy E_f belonging to a continuous part of the spectrum of H_0. In this case the probability of transition at time t, $|\langle \varphi_f | \psi(t) \rangle|^2$, is actually a probability density. That is, we must integrate the probability density over a range of final states in order to give a physical prediction. The time-dependent perturbation theory can be applied to this situation.

Remember

One very important result is *Fermi's golden rule*. This formula relates to the case of a constant perturbation. It can be demonstrated that in this case, transitions can occur only between states of equal energies. The probability density P_{fi} of transition from $|\varphi_i\rangle$ to $|\varphi_j\rangle$ increases linearly with time, and

$$W_{fi} = \frac{dP_{fi}(t)}{dt} = \frac{2\pi}{\hbar}\left|\langle \psi_f | W(t) | \psi_i \rangle\right|^2 \rho(E_f)$$

where $\rho(E_f)$ is the density of final states.

Chapter 11
OTHER APPROXIMATION METHODS

IN THIS CHAPTER:

✔ *The Variational Method*
✔ *The WKB Approximation*

The Variational Method

The perturbation theory studied in Chapter 10 is not the only approximation method in quantum mechanics. In this section, we present another method applicable to conservative systems. Consider a physical system with time-independent hamiltonian H. We assume for simplicity that the entire spectrum of H is discrete and nondegenerate:

$$H|\varphi_n\rangle = E_n|\varphi_n\rangle$$

We denote by E_0 the smallest eigenvalue of H. An arbitrary state $|\psi\rangle$ can be written in the form

$$|\psi\rangle = \sum_n c_n|\varphi_n\rangle$$

Then we can find the expectation value of H in this state

$$\langle\psi|H|\psi\rangle = \sum_n |c_n|^2 E_n \geq E_0 \sum_n |c_n|^2$$

Important!

After normalizing we obtain

$$\langle H \rangle = \frac{\langle \psi | H | \psi \rangle}{\langle \psi | \psi \rangle} \geq E_0$$

This is the basis of the variational method: choosing absolutely any trial wave function, the expectation value of the hamiltonian will always be greater than or equal to the actual ground state energy, and so we obtain an upper bound.

A family of kets $|\psi(\alpha)\rangle$ is chosen, called *trial kets*. The mean value of H in these states is calculated, and the expression $\langle H(\alpha) \rangle$ is minimized with respect to the parameter α. The minimal value obtained is an approximation of the ground state energy E_0.

This is actually a part of a more general result called the *Ritz theorem*: the mean value of the hamiltonian H is stationary in the neighborhood of its discrete eigenvalues. The variational method can therefore be generalized to provide estimations for other energy levels. If the function $\langle H(\alpha) \rangle$ obtained from the trial kets has several extrema, they give approximate values of some of its energies E_n.

Solved Problem 11.1

(a) Using the variational method, estimate the ground-state energy of a hydrogen atom. Choose as trial functions the spherically symmetric functions

$$\varphi_\alpha(r) = \begin{cases} C\left(1 - \dfrac{r}{\alpha}\right) & \text{for } r \leq \alpha \\ 0 & \text{for } r > \alpha \end{cases}$$

where C is a normalization constant and α is the variational parameter.

(b) Find the extremum value of α. Compare this value with the Bohr radius a_0.

Solution.

(a) First we compute the normalization constant. This gives

$$C^2 = \frac{15}{\pi\alpha^3}$$

The kinetic energy is given by

$$\langle E_k \rangle = \frac{-2\pi\hbar^2}{2m} \int_0^\alpha r^2 \varphi_\alpha(r) \left[\frac{1}{r} \frac{d^2(r\varphi_\alpha)}{dr^2} \right] dr$$

Integration by parts gives

$$\langle E_k \rangle = \frac{-\pi\hbar^2}{m} \left(r\varphi_\alpha(r) \frac{d(r\varphi_\alpha)}{dr} \right)\Bigg|_0^\alpha + \frac{\pi\hbar^2}{m} \int_0^\alpha \left[\frac{d(r\varphi_\alpha)}{dr} \right]^2 dr$$

But since

$$\left. (r\varphi_\alpha(r)) \right|_0 = 0 = \left. (r\varphi_\alpha(r)) \right|_\alpha$$

the first term vanishes and we have

$$\langle E_k \rangle = \frac{15\hbar^2}{2m\alpha^3} \int_0^\alpha \left[1 - \frac{2r}{\alpha} \right]^2 dr = \frac{5\hbar^2}{m\alpha^2}$$

The potential energy is

$$\langle V \rangle = 2\pi \int_0^\infty r^2 \varphi_\alpha(r) V(r) \varphi_\alpha(r) dr = 2\pi ke^2 \int_0^\alpha r |\varphi_\alpha(r)|^2 dr = \frac{-5ke^2}{2\alpha}$$

Thus the total energy as a function of α is

$$\langle E(\alpha) \rangle = 5 \left(\frac{\hbar^2}{m\alpha^2} - \frac{ke^2}{2\alpha} \right)$$

(b) The extremum condition

$$\frac{d\langle E \rangle}{d\alpha} = 0$$

leads to

$$\frac{2\hbar^2}{3\alpha_0^3} = \frac{ke^2}{2\alpha_0^2}$$

or

$$\alpha_0 = \frac{4\hbar^2}{kme^2} = 4a_0$$

The WKB Approximation

Apart from the perturbation and variational methods described earlier, there is another method that is suitable for obtaining solutions to the one-dimensional Schrödinger equation. This is called the semiclassical or WKB approximation (named for Wentzel, Kramers, and Brillouin). The WKB method can also be applied to higher-dimensional problems if the potential is spherically symmetric and a radial differential equation can be separated.

The WKB method introduces an expansion in powers of $\hbar$ in which terms of order higher than $\hbar^2$ are neglected. Thus, one replaces the Schrödinger equation by its classical limit $\hbar \to 0$. However, the method can be applied even in regions in which the classical interpretation is meaningless.

Consider the Schrödinger equation in one dimension:

$$\frac{d^2\psi}{dx^2} + \frac{2m}{\hbar^2} \left[E - V(x) \right] \psi = 0$$

We consider only stationary states and write the wave function in the form

$$\psi(x) = e^{iu(x)}$$

We shall use the abbreviation

$$k(x) = \begin{cases} \dfrac{1}{\hbar}\sqrt{2m\left[E - V(x)\right]} & \text{for} \quad E > V(x) \\[4mm] \dfrac{-i}{\hbar}\sqrt{2m\left[V(x) - E\right]} & \text{for} \quad E < V(x) \end{cases}$$

Substituting ψ into the Schrödinger equation, one finds that $u(x)$ satisfies the equation

$$i\frac{d^2u}{dx^2} - \left(\frac{du}{dx}\right)^2 + \left[k(x)\right]^2 = 0$$

⭐ **Note!**

In the WKB approximation we expand $u(x)$ in powers of $\hbar$:

$$u(x) = u_0 + \frac{\hbar}{i}u_1 + \left(\frac{\hbar}{i}\right)^2 u_2 + \cdots$$

and we consider only the lowest orders, u_0, u_1. We obtain the approximate wave function

$$\psi(x) = \frac{C_1}{\sqrt{|k(x)|}} e^{i\int k(x')dx'} + \frac{C_2}{\sqrt{|k(x)|}} e^{-i\int k(x')dx'}$$

A region in which $E > V(x)$ is called a *classically allowed region* of motion, while a region in which $E < V(x)$ is called *classically inaccessible*.

The points in the boundary between these two kinds of regions are called *turning points*.

The WKB approximation is based on the condition

$$\frac{1}{2}\left|k'(x)\right| << \left|k^2(x)\right|$$

This condition can be expressed in a number of equivalent forms. Using the de Broglie wavelength, $\lambda = \dfrac{2\pi}{k}$, we can write it as

$$\frac{\lambda}{4\pi}\left|\frac{dk}{dx}\right| << k$$

Adjacent to the turning points, for which $k(x_0) = 0$, we have

$$k \approx \left.\frac{dk}{dx}\right|_{x_0}(x - x_0)$$

Thus the semiclassical approximation is applicable for a distance from the turning point satisfying the condition

$$\left|x - x_0\right| >> \frac{\lambda}{4\pi}$$

Consider a turning point. Assume that except in its immediate neighborhood the WKB approximation is applicable. The matching between the WKB approximations on each side of the turning point depends on whether the classical region is to the left or to the right. If it is to the left, then for $x > b$

$$\psi_1(x) = \frac{A_1}{\sqrt{k}}\cos\left(\int_b^x k(x')\,dx' - B_1\pi\right)$$

If it is to the right, then for $x < a$

$$\psi_2(x) = \frac{A_2}{\sqrt{k}}\cos\left(\int_x^a k(x')\,dx' - B_2\pi\right)$$

The WKB approximation can be applied to derive an equation for the energies of a bound state. Using the connection formulas in each side of the potential well one obtains

$$\int_a^b k(x)\,dx = \left(n + \frac{1}{2}\right)\pi$$

This equation is called the *Bohr-Sommerfeld quantization rule*.

If one considers a potential barrier of the form $V(x)$ between $x = a$ and $x = b$ and a particle with energy E, the transmission coefficient in the WKB approximation is given by

$$T \approx \exp\left[\frac{-2}{\hbar}\int_a^b \sqrt{2m[V(x) - E]}\,dx\right]$$

Solved Problem 11.2 Use the WKB approximation to obtain the energy levels of a linear harmonic oscillator.

Solution. Consider the Bohr-Sommerfeld quantization rule:

$$\int_a^b p(x)\,dx = \left(n + \frac{1}{2}\right)\hbar\pi$$

where

$$p(x) = \sqrt{2m[E - V(x)]}$$

is the momentum of the oscillator, E its energy, and $V(x)$ its potential energy. Since

$$\oint p\,dx = 2\int_a^b p\,dx$$

holds for a linear harmonic oscillator, we may write the Bohr-Sommerfeld quantization rule in the form above. For the harmonic oscillator, we have $V = \dfrac{1}{2} m\omega^2 x^2$. The points a and b are the turning points that are determined by the condition $p(a) = p(b) = 0$ or $E - V = 0$; thus,

$$E - \frac{1}{2} m\omega^2 x^2 = 0$$

So, we have

$$a = -\sqrt{\frac{2E}{m\omega^2}}$$

$$b = \sqrt{\frac{2E}{m\omega^2}}$$

We introduce the new variable

$$z = x\sqrt{\frac{m\omega^2}{2E}}$$

and obtain

$$\int_a^b p(x)\,dx = \frac{2E}{\omega} \int_{-1}^{1} \sqrt{1 - z^2}\,dz = \frac{\pi E}{\omega}$$

Comparing this result to the Bohr-Sommerfeld rule gives

$$E_n = \hbar\omega\left(n + \frac{1}{2} \right)$$

Thus, in the case of the linear harmonic oscillator, the WKB approximation gives the exact answer.

Chapter 12
NUMERICAL METHODS

IN THIS CHAPTER:

✔ *Numerical Quadrature*
✔ *Roots*
✔ *Integration of Ordinary Differential Equations*

Numerical Quadrature

The *numerical quadrature* of the definite integral of a function $f(x)$ between two limits a and b is accomplished by dividing the interval $[a,b]$ into N small intervals, between $N + 1$ points denoted by

$$a = x_0, x_1, \ldots, x_N = b$$

The points x_i are equally spaced apart using a constant step

$$h = \frac{(b - a)}{N}$$

so that

$$x_i = x_0 + ih \text{ where } i = 0, 1, \ldots, N$$

The basic idea behind quadrature is to write the integral as the sum of integrals over small intervals

$$\int_a^b f(x)\,dx = \int_a^{a+h} f(x)\,dx + \int_{a+h}^{a+2h} f(x)\,dx + \cdots$$

and in these small intervals approximate $f(x)$ by a function that can be integrated exactly.

We will demonstrate two methods of quadrature. The first method is called the *trapezoidal method*; it is based on the approximation of $f(x)$ to a linear function. In this case, the integral

$$\int_{x_i}^{x_{i+1}} f(x)\,dx = \left[f\left(x_{i+1}\right) + f\left(x_i\right) \right]\frac{h}{2}$$

(each region is shaped like a trapezoid) so if we denote $f(x_i) = f_i$ we obtain

$$\int_a^b f(x)\,dx = h\left[\frac{1}{2}f_0 + f_1 + f_2 + \cdots + f_{N-1} + \frac{1}{2}f_N \right]$$

The second method is called *Simpson's method* and is based on the approximation of $f(x)$ to a second-degree polynomial on three points. In this case the integral

$$\int_{x_i}^{x_{i+2}} f(x)\,dx \approx h\left[\frac{1}{3}f_i + \frac{4}{3}f_{i+1} + \frac{1}{3}f_{i+2} \right]$$

so that for the whole interval

$$\int_a^b f(x)\,dx \approx \frac{h}{3}\left[f_0 + 4f_1 + 2f_2 + 4f_3 + \cdots + f_N \right]$$

One should be constantly aware of the fact that these methods are only an approximation of the exact integral.

You Need to Know ✔

These approximations are improved as we consider larger N; however, very large N will slow computations. Therefore, it is preferable to choose N to give an appropriate amount of precision. In the trapezoidal method, the approximation error is proportional to $1/N^2$, while in Simpson's method it is proportional to $1/N^4$.

Roots

In order to determine the roots of a function, $f(x)$, we must solve the equation $f(x) = 0$. All numerical methods for finding roots depend on one or more initial guesses, and each algorithm approximates the root after a given number of iterations. Note that by initial guess we do not necessarily mean a close guess for the root, though the better a guess is, the faster the convergence will be (and fewer iterations will be needed). Thus, to obtain the initial guess for a given root of the function, it is helpful to first plot the function.

We describe three methods for finding roots. The first is called the *bisection method*. This method is useful when we know that the root we seek is found in a specific interval, say $[x_1, x_2]$. In this case, we know that the signs of $f(x_1)$ and $f(x_2)$ are opposite. In the first iteration we evaluate $f(x)$ at the midpoint between x_1 and x_2; then we use the midpoint to replace the limit with the same sign. In each successive iteration the interval containing  the root gets smaller by a factor of one-half, so the maximal error in our estimation is simply half the interval between the new limits. Thus we need $n = \log(\varepsilon_0/\varepsilon)$ iterations to obtain the root with maximal error of $\varepsilon/2$. Note that ε_0 is the initial interval. The bisection method will always converge if the initial interval contains a root.

The second algorithm, the *Newton-Raphson method*, uses the derivative $f'(x)$ at an arbitrary point x. We begin with an initial guess x^1. Each new approximation for the root depends on the previous one

$$x^{i+1} = x^i - \frac{f\left(x^i\right)}{f'\left(x^i\right)}$$

We stop when the value of

$$\left|x^{i+1} - x^i\right|$$

is less than the tolerance we have preset. To understand how the method works, we write the formula above as

$$f(x^i) + f'(x^i)\,(x^{i+1} - x^i) = 0$$

Notice that the left-hand side of this is a linear extrapolation to the value of $f(x^{i+1})$, which should be zero.

The third method, called the *secant method*, is similar to the Newton-Raphson method. Here we do not evaluate the derivative but use the approximation

$$f'\left(x^i\right) = \frac{f\left(x^i\right) - f\left(x^{i-1}\right)}{x^i - x^{i-1}}$$

Hence we obtain

$$x^{i+1} = x^i - \frac{f\left(x^i\right)}{f'\left(x^i\right)}$$

with the approximated derivative given above.

Integration of Ordinary Differential Equations

Solving differential equations is of paramount importance in physics. Many key results of physics are formulated in terms of differential equations. We introduce several methods for solving differential equations of the form

$$\frac{dy}{dx} = f(x, y)$$

The methods differ in their accuracy, and in the time needed to obtain the required accuracy. One should decide which method to use according to these criteria. Note that higher-order differential equations such as

$$\frac{d^2y}{dx^2} = F(x, y)$$

can be written as

$$\frac{dz}{dx} = F(x, y)$$

$$z = \frac{dy}{dx}$$

Thus they can be solved using the same methods.

The first method, the *Euler method*, is the simplest and least accurate method. We approximate the differential equation as a difference equation

$$\frac{\Delta y}{\Delta x} = f(x, y)$$

We iterate the value of $y(x)$ from a starting point $y_0 = y(x_0)$ by

$$y_{n+1} = y_n + f(x_n, y_n)(x_{n+1} - x_n) = y_n + f(x_n, y_n)h$$

where h is the constant-size step in x. Each point depends only on the previous point.

The second method, the *Runge-Kutta method*, is based on the Euler method using an approximation of $f(x,y)$ by a given order of the Taylor series expansion. The higher the order of the Taylor expansion, the better the accuracy. Consider the second-order Runge-Kutta method:

$$y_{n+1} = y_n + k_2$$
$$k_1 = hf(x_n, y_n)$$
$$k_2 = hf\left(x_n + \frac{h}{2}, y_n + \frac{k_1}{2}\right)$$

Similarly, the third-order Runge-Kutta method is

$$y_{n+1} = y_n + \frac{1}{6}\left(k_1 + 4k_2 + k_3\right)$$

$$k_1 = hf\left(x_n, y_n\right)$$

$$k_2 = hf\left(x_n + \frac{h}{2}, y_n + \frac{k_1}{2}\right)$$

$$k_3 = hf\left(x_n + h, y_n - k_1 + 2k_2\right)$$

The Schrödinger equation is a second-order differential equation. Thus, the methods described above need as an initial condition the value of the wave function and its derivative at a given point. Since the value of the derivative of the wave function is usually not given, we are left only with the value of the wave function at two points (the boundaries). We demonstrate here an algorithm to solve second-order differential equations with two boundary conditions—the *Numerov algorithm.*

Numerov's method is used to solve a differential equation of the form

$$\frac{d^2 y}{dx^2} + k^2\left(x\right)y = S\left(x\right)$$

We approximate the second derivative by the three-point difference formula

$$\frac{y_{n+1} - 2y_n + y_{n-1}}{h^2} = y_n'' + \frac{h^2}{12}y_n''''$$

where the second and fourth derivatives at point x_n are used.

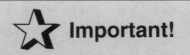 **Important!**

The error in the Euler method approximation is proportional to h^2.

Second-order Runge-Kutta method has an error proportional to h^3.

The third-order Runge-Kutta method has an error proportional to h^4.

The error in the Numerov algorithm is proportional to h^6.

Chapter 13
IDENTICAL PARTICLES

IN THIS CHAPTER:

- ✔ *Introduction*
- ✔ *Symmetries of Wave Functions*
- ✔ *Bosons and Fermions*

Introduction

Suppose you have a basketball and your friend has a soccer ball with the same mass; you kick them towards each other, simultaneously, with the same velocity. Two things could happen: (a) The balls collide and each goes back to its owner (b) The balls travel through parallel paths without touching and exchange hands. Since the balls have different shapes and colors, you can tell the difference. But if the balls were identical, it would be harder to tell. When we  consider identical quantum particles, the situation gets even worse because we cannot even trace the trajectories of the particles. In this chapter we examine the special properties of a system composed of identical particles.

Symmetries of Wave Functions

We say that particles of a system are *identical* (or *indistinguishable*) if no observer can detect any permutation of these particles.

117

The property of indistinguishability gives rise to *symmetries* in the system. Consider a system of n identical particles with the eigenvector $|\varphi_i\rangle$ for the particle i ($i = 1,...,n$). We denote the state of the system by a vector of these eigenvectors, keeping in mind that different ordering of the $|\varphi_i\rangle$ corresponds to two different vectors, e.g., if $n = 2$ then

$$(|\varphi_1\rangle,|\varphi_2\rangle) \neq (|\varphi_2\rangle,|\varphi_1\rangle)$$

If σ is a *permutation* on the indices, then it can be written as

$$\sigma = \begin{pmatrix} 1 & 2 & 3 & \cdots & n \\ \sigma(1) & \sigma(2) & \sigma(3) & \cdots & \sigma(n) \end{pmatrix}$$

meaning that the vector $(1,2,...,n)$ becomes $(|\sigma_1\rangle,|\sigma_2\rangle,...,|\sigma_n\rangle)$ after the action of σ. Thus σ permutes the eigenvectors

$$\sigma(|\varphi_1\rangle,...,|\varphi_n\rangle) = (|\varphi_{\sigma(1)}\rangle,...,|\varphi_{\sigma(n)}\rangle)$$

One can see that σ acts as a linear operator. A permutation σ may be written as a product of *transpositions*, i.e., permutations that swap two numbers. If the decomposition of σ consists of an even number of transpositions, then σ is called an even permutation, and we write $\mathrm{sgn}(\sigma) = 1$, and if this number is odd, then σ is called an odd permutation denoted $\mathrm{sgn}(\sigma) = -1$. The vector

$$|u\rangle = |\varphi_1\rangle,...,|\varphi_n\rangle$$

is said to be *symmetric* if

$$\sigma|u\rangle = |u\rangle$$

for an arbitrary permutation. The same vector is said to be *antisymmetric* if

$$\sigma|u\rangle = \mathrm{sgn}(\sigma)|u\rangle$$

for an arbitrary permutation. We define two operators

$$S = \frac{1}{n!} \sum_{\sigma\, permutation} \sigma$$

$$A = \frac{1}{n!} \sum_{\sigma\, permutation} (\text{sgn}\,\sigma)\sigma$$

Remember

S and A project the entire space of wave functions, *H*, on two subspaces: the space of symmetric wave functions, a_S, and the space of antisymmetric wave functions, a_A:

$$Hs = SH$$
$$H_A = AH$$

and in addition

$$H = H_A \oplus H_S$$

that is, every vector is a unique sum of a completely symmetric vector and a completely antisymmetric vector.

An arbitrary antisymmetric wave function can be written

$$|u_A\rangle = A|u\rangle$$

for any wave function

$$|u\rangle = (|\varphi_1\rangle, ..., |\varphi_n\rangle)$$

Hence if $\{|\varphi^{(j)}\rangle\}$ is a basis of the single-particle space of states, then a basis of the antisymmetric space of all n particles is given by applying A on a basis of the entire space, spanned by $|\varphi^{j_1}\rangle, ..., |\varphi^{j_n}\rangle$; thus

$$\left|\alpha_{j_1,...,j_n}\right\rangle = A\left(\left|\varphi_1^{j_1}\right\rangle, ..., \left|\varphi_n^{j_n}\right\rangle\right) = \sum_{\sigma} \frac{1}{n!}(\text{sgn }\sigma)\left(\left|\varphi_1^{j_{\sigma(1)}}\right\rangle, ..., \left|\varphi_n^{j_{\sigma(n)}}\right\rangle\right)$$

$$\left|\alpha_{j_1,...,j_n}\right\rangle = \frac{1}{n!}\begin{vmatrix} \left|\varphi_1^{j_1}\right\rangle & \left|\varphi_1^{j_2}\right\rangle & \cdots & \left|\varphi_1^{j_n}\right\rangle \\ \left|\varphi_2^{j_1}\right\rangle & \left|\varphi_2^{j_2}\right\rangle & \cdots & \vdots \\ \vdots & \vdots & \ddots & \vdots \\ \left|\varphi_n^{j_1}\right\rangle & \cdots & \cdots & \left|\varphi_n^{j_n}\right\rangle \end{vmatrix}$$

is a basis of H_A. The last equality comes from the properties of the determinant. This determinant is known as *Slater's determinant* and is the solution for the Schrödinger equation for non-interacting fermions.

Bosons and Fermions

From experimental observations it seems there are two kinds of particles. The first kind consists of particles that have completely symmetric wave functions; they are known as *bosons*. The second kind consists of particles with completely antisymmetric wave functions; they are called *fermions*. There are no particles with mixed symmetry. *Pauli's exclusion principle*, a basic principle that is valid only for identical particles that are fermions, states that two identical fermions cannot be in the same quantum state. An alternative formulation of this principle asserts that the probability of finding two identical fermions with the same quantum numbers is zero.

Solved Problem 13.1 The symmetrization postulate for fermions states that the wave function of a group of n identical fermions is completely antisymmetric. Use this to derive the Pauli exclusion principle.

Solution. The matrix $|\alpha_{j_1,...,j_n}\rangle$ above could represent these fermions. If two of these fermions were in the same quantum state, two columns of this matrix would be the same, forcing the determinant to vanish; consequently, no nontrivial wave function exists in this case.

Solved Problem 13.2 Show explicitly that Slater's determinant for two fermions is antisymmetric.

Solution. The Slater determinant for two fermions is given by

$$\left| u\left(1,2\right) \right\rangle = \frac{1}{2!} \begin{vmatrix} \left| \varphi_1^{j_1} \right\rangle & \left| \varphi_1^{j_2} \right\rangle \\ \left| \varphi_2^{j_1} \right\rangle & \left| \varphi_2^{j_2} \right\rangle \end{vmatrix} = \frac{1}{2}\left(\left| \varphi_1^{j_1} \right\rangle \left| \varphi_2^{j_2} \right\rangle - \left| \varphi_1^{j_2} \right\rangle \left| \varphi_2^{j_1} \right\rangle \right)$$

and

$$\left| u\left(2,1\right) \right\rangle = \frac{1}{2}\left(\left| \varphi_1^{j_2} \right\rangle \left| \varphi_2^{j_1} \right\rangle - \left| \varphi_1^{j_1} \right\rangle \left| \varphi_2^{j_2} \right\rangle \right)$$

Thus $\left| u(1,2) \right\rangle = -\left| u(2,1) \right\rangle$

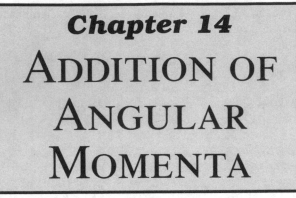

Chapter 14

ADDITION OF ANGULAR MOMENTA

Introduction

Consider two angular momenta, $\vec{j}_1$ and $\vec{j}_2$. These momenta can be angular momenta relating to two different particles or to one particle (orbital and spin angular momentum). These two momenta act in different state spaces, so that all their components are commuting with one another. The individual states of $\vec{j}_1$ and $\vec{j}_2$ will be denoted, as usual, as $|j_1, m_1\rangle$ and $|j_2, m_2\rangle$.

Don't Forget!

The operators, eigenvectors, and eigenvalues are related by

$$j_1^2|j_1,m_1\rangle = j_1(j_1 + 1)\hbar^2|j_1,m_1\rangle$$
$$j_{1z}|j_1,m_1\rangle = m_1\hbar|j_1,m_1\rangle$$

and similarly for $\vec{j}_2$. The state space of the compound system is obtained by taking the direct product (tensor product) of the individual state space of the two angular momenta,

$$|j_1,m_1\rangle \otimes |j_2,m_2\rangle = |j_1,j_2;m_1,m_2\rangle \equiv |m_1,m_2\rangle$$

For fixed $\vec{j}_1$ and $\vec{j}_2$, m_1 and m_2 have the values

$$m_1 = -j_1,-j_1 + 1,...,j_1$$
$$m_2 = -j_2,-j_2 + 1,...,j_2$$

where the set of numbers $\{j_1,m_1\}$ and $\{j_2,m_2\}$ are either integers or half-integers.

The state space of the compound system is $(2j_1 + 1)(2j_2 + 1)$-dimensional space. The states $|m_1,m_2\rangle$ are, according to their constructions, eigenstates of the operators $\{j_1^2,j_2^2,j_{1z},j_{2z}\}$.

The $\{j_1^2,j_2^2,J^2,J_z\}$ Basis

In the absence of interaction between $\vec{j}_1$ and $\vec{j}_2$, the operators commute with the hamiltonian and thus $|j_1,m_1\rangle$ and $|j_2,m_2\rangle$ are also eigenstates of the system. However, if $\vec{j}_1$ and $\vec{j}_2$ interact with

$$H = H_0 + \alpha\,\vec{j}_1 \cdot \vec{j}_2$$

where α is a coupling constant, then $\vec{j}_1$ and $\vec{j}_2$ are not conserved, but $\vec{j} = \vec{j}_1 + \vec{j}_2$ is conserved. The eigenstates in this basis will be denoted by $|j_1,j_2,J,M\rangle \equiv |J,M\rangle$.

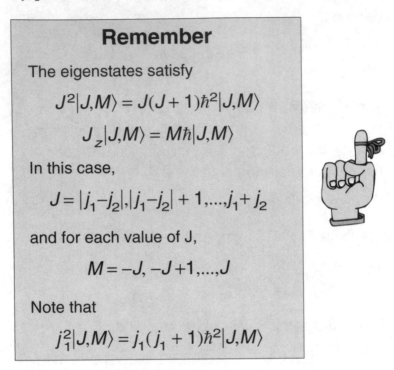

Remember

The eigenstates satisfy

$$J^2|J,M\rangle = J(J+1)\hbar^2|J,M\rangle$$

$$J_z|J,M\rangle = M\hbar|J,M\rangle$$

In this case,

$$J = |j_1-j_2|, |j_1-j_2| + 1,\ldots,j_1+j_2$$

and for each value of J,

$$M = -J, -J+1,\ldots,J$$

Note that

$$j_1^2|J,M\rangle = j_1(j_1 + 1)\hbar^2|J,M\rangle$$

Therefore, using the identity

$$2\vec{j}_1 \cdot \vec{j}_2 = J^2 - j_1^2 - j_2^2$$

we have

$$\vec{j}_1 \cdot \vec{j}_2 |J,M\rangle = \frac{\hbar^2}{2}\left[J(J+1) - j_1(j_1+1) - j_2(j_2+1)\right]|J,M\rangle$$

As a result, $|J,M\rangle$ are also eigenstates of the operators $\vec{j}_1 \cdot \vec{j}_2$. In a commonly employed terminology, one refers to $|J,M\rangle$ as an eigenstate in the *coupled representation* and to $|m_1,m_2\rangle$ as an eigenstate in the *uncoupled representation*.

Clebsch-Gordan Coefficients

The two sets of orthonormal states $|m_1,m_2\rangle$ and $|J,M\rangle$ are related by a unitary transformation.

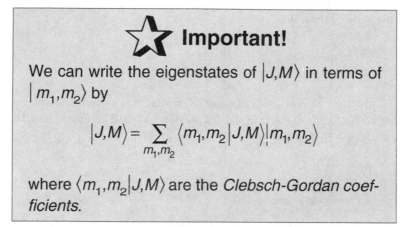

⭐ **Important!**

We can write the eigenstates of $|J,M\rangle$ in terms of $|m_1,m_2\rangle$ by

$$|J,M\rangle = \sum_{m_1,m_2} \langle m_1,m_2|J,M\rangle|m_1,m_2\rangle$$

where $\langle m_1,m_2|J,M\rangle$ are the *Clebsch-Gordan coefficients*.

It is possible to obtain a general expression for these coefficients; however, it is often simpler to construct the coefficients for particular cases. The can be calculated by successive applications of $J_\pm = J_x \pm iJ_y$ on the vectors $|J,M\rangle$, using the following relations:

$$J_\pm|J,M\rangle = \hbar\sqrt{J(J+1) - M(M\pm1)}|J,M\pm1\rangle$$

$$J_{1\pm}|m_1,m_2\rangle = \hbar\sqrt{J_1(J_1+1) - m_1(m_1\pm1)}|m_1\pm1,m_2\rangle$$

together with the *phase condition*,

$$|J = J_1 + J_2, M = \pm(j_1 + j_2)\rangle = |m_1 = \pm j_1, m_2 = \pm j_2\rangle$$

It is useful to remember that

$$\langle m_1,m_2|J,M\rangle = 0$$

unless $M = m_1 + m_2$, and it's real in any case.

Solved Problem 14.1 Two angular momenta of respective magnitudes j_1 and j_2 and total angular momentum $\vec{J} = \vec{j}_1 + \vec{j}_2$ are described by the basis $|m_1,m_2\rangle \equiv |j_1,m_1\rangle \otimes |j_2,m_2\rangle$. By construction, the states $|m_1,m_2\rangle$ are eigenstates of $\{j_1^2 j_2^2, J_{1z}, J_{2z}\}$ and $J_z = J_{1z} + J_{2z}$.

(a) Find all the eigenvalues of the operator J_z and their degrees of degeneracy.

(b) Consider the states

$$|\psi_+\rangle = |m_1 = j_1, m_2 = j_2\rangle$$
$$|\psi_-\rangle = |m_1 = -j_1, m_2 = -j_2\rangle$$

for which m_1 and m_2 both assume either maximal or minimal values. Show that the states $|\psi_\pm\rangle$ are eigenstates of J^2 (as well as J_z) and find the corresponding eigenvalues.

Solution.

(a) The basis states satisfy

$$j_1^2|m_1,m_2\rangle = j_1(j_1+1)\hbar^2|m_1,m_2\rangle$$
$$j_2^2|m_1,m_2\rangle = j_2(j_2+1)\hbar^2|m_1,m_2\rangle$$

where j_1 and j_2 are fixed quantum numbers and

$$J_{1z}|m_1,m_2\rangle = m_1\hbar|m_1,m_2\rangle$$
$$J_{2z}|m_1,m_2\rangle = m_2\hbar|m_1,m_2\rangle$$

where m_1 and m_2 are either integers or half-integers. We use these to immediately find

$$J_z|m_1,m_2\rangle = (J_{1z} + J_{2z})|m_1,m_2\rangle = (m_1 + m_2)\hbar|m_1,m_2\rangle = M\hbar|m_1,m_2\rangle$$

Consequently, the eigenvalues of J_z are $M\hbar$ where the quantum number $M = m_1 + m_2$ takes the values

$$M = -(j_1 + j_2), -(j_1 + j_2) + 1, \dots, j_1 + j_2$$

The degree of degeneracy, $g(M)$, of these values has the following properties:

    1. The value $M = M_{max} = j_1 + j_2$ is not degenerate, $g(j_1 + j_2) = 1$.

    2. The degree of degeneracy is increased by 1 as M decreases by 1 until a maximum degeneracy is reached for the value $M = j_1 - j_2$. The degeneracy remains constant as long as $M \le |j_1 - j_2|$ and is equal to $g(M) = 2j_2 + 1$ in this region.

    3. For $M < -(j_1 - j_2)$, the degeneracy decreases by 1 as M decreases by 1. The value of $M = M_{min} = -(j_1 + j_2)$ is not degenerate. Generally, $g(M) = g(-M)$.

(b) From the above, the states $|\psi_\pm\rangle$ are eigenvectors of J_z with eigenvalues $\lambda_\pm = \pm\hbar(j_1 + j_2)$. Since the operators J_z and J^2 commute, we have

$$J_z J^2 |\psi_\pm\rangle = J^2(J_z|\psi_\pm\rangle) = \lambda_\pm(J^2|\psi_\pm\rangle)$$

Consequently, the vectors $J^2|\psi_\pm\rangle$ are also eigenvectors of J_z with the same eigenvalues, $\lambda_\pm$. However, because of the nondegeneracy of the $\lambda_\pm$, the eigenvectors $J^2|\psi_\pm\rangle$ must be proportional to $|\psi_\pm\rangle$, so that $|\psi_\pm\rangle$ are eigenvectors of J^2 as well as J_z. Indeed, since $|\psi_\pm\rangle$ both correspond to the extreme possible values of m_1 and m_2,

$$J^2|\psi_\pm\rangle = (J_1^2 + J_2^2 + 2J_{1z}J_{2z} + J_{1+}J_{2-} + J_{1-}J_{2+})\,|\psi_\pm\rangle$$
$$J^2|\psi_\pm\rangle = [(j_1 + j_2) + (j_1 + j_2 + 1)]\hbar^2|\psi_\pm\rangle$$

Thus $|\psi_\pm\rangle$ both correspond to the same eigenvalue of J^2 given by $J(J+1)\hbar^2$.

Solved Problem 14.2 Let $\vec{S} = \vec{S}_1 + \vec{S}_2$ be the total angular momentum of two spin 1/2 particles. Calculate the Clebsch-Gordan coefficients by successive applications of $S_\pm$ on the vectors $|S,m\rangle$. Work separately in the two subspaces, $S = 1$ and $S = 0$.

Solution. The states $|S = S_1 + S_2, m = \pm(S_1 + S_2)\rangle$ are eigenstates of S^2 and S_z with nondegenerate eigenvalues $\lambda_\pm = \pm\hbar(S_1 + S_2)$. Therefore,

$$|S = S_1 + S_2, m = \pm(S_1 + S_2)\rangle = e^{i\varphi}|m_1 = \pm S_1, m_2 = \pm S_2\rangle$$

contains a phase, φ, which we may choose to be zero. Consider the $S = 1$ subspace and notice that our choice of phase convention gives

$$|1,1\rangle = |+,+\rangle$$

Operate with $S_- = S_{1-} + S_{2-}$ on both sides of this equation and use the eigenvalue equations:

$$S_-|1,1\rangle = \hbar\sqrt{2}|1,0\rangle$$

$$\left(S_{1-} + S_{2-}\right)|+,+\rangle = \hbar\sqrt{1}|-,+\rangle + \hbar\sqrt{1}|+,-\rangle$$

Therefore,

$$|1,0\rangle = \frac{1}{\sqrt{2}}\left(|-,+\rangle + |+,-\rangle\right)$$

Similarly, operate with S_- on $|1,0\rangle$

$$S_-|1,0\rangle = \hbar\sqrt{2}|1,-1\rangle$$

$$\left(S_{1-} + S_{2-}\right)\frac{1}{\sqrt{2}}\left(|-,+\rangle + |+,-\rangle\right) = \frac{\hbar}{\sqrt{2}}\left[|-,-\rangle + |-,-\rangle\right] = \sqrt{2}\hbar|-,-\rangle$$

which leads to

$$|1,-1\rangle = |-,-\rangle$$

Next consider the $S = 0$ subspace where $m = 0 = m_1 + m_2$. In general we can write a linear superposition

$$|0,0\rangle = \alpha|+,-\rangle + \beta|-,+\rangle$$

We can use the orthonormality of the $|S,m\rangle$ to find

$$\langle 1,0 \mid 0,0\rangle = 0$$

so that

$$\frac{1}{\sqrt{2}}(\alpha + \beta) = 0$$

and

$$\langle 0,0 \mid 0,0 \rangle = 1$$

so that

$$|\alpha|^2 + |\beta|^2 = 1$$

gives us

$$\alpha = -\beta = \frac{1}{\sqrt{2}}$$

Therefore,

$$|0,0\rangle = \frac{1}{\sqrt{2}}\left(|+,-\rangle - |-,+\rangle\right)$$

Notice that all of the $S = 1$ states are symmetric under particle exchange, but the $S = 0$ state is antisymmetric.

Solved Problem 14.3 Consider a system of two spin $1/2$ particles whose orbital variables are ignored. The hamiltonian of the system is $H = \varepsilon_1 \sigma_{1z} + \varepsilon_2 \sigma_{2z}$, where ε_i are real constants and σ_{iz} are the projection of the spins $\vec{S}_i = \frac{\hbar}{2}\vec{\sigma}_i$ of the two particles onto the z axis.

(a) The initial state of the system, at time $t = 0$ is $|\psi(0)\rangle = \frac{1}{\sqrt{2}}(|+,-\rangle + |-,+\rangle)$. $S^2 = (\vec{S}_1 + \vec{S}_2)^2$ is measured at time t. What are the values that can be arrived at and what are their probabilities?

(b) If the initial state of the system is arbitrary, what Bohr frequencies might appear in the evolution of $\langle S^2 \rangle$?

Solution.

(a) The eigenstates of S^2 are the $|S,m\rangle$ states, where $S = 1,0$ corresponds to the triplet and singlet states, respectively. The results of the measurements of S^2 are $2\hbar^2$ for the triplet states and zero for the singlet state. However, the states $|S,m\rangle$ are not eigenstates of the hamiltonian, and consequently the probabilities are changing as a function of time. The stationary states of the system are

$$\{|+,+\rangle,|+,-\rangle,|-,+\rangle,|-,-\rangle\}$$

and its energy levels are given by $\pm\varepsilon_1\pm\varepsilon_2$. Therefore, taking into account the initial state of the system, $|\psi(0)\rangle = |1,0\rangle$, and using the time-evolution postulate, we find

$$|\psi(t)\rangle = \frac{1}{\sqrt{2}}\left[e^{-i(\varepsilon_1-\varepsilon_2)t/\hbar}|+,-\rangle + e^{i(\varepsilon_1-\varepsilon_2)t/\hbar}|-,+\rangle\right]$$

Now express these states in terms of $|S,m\rangle$:

$$|+,-\rangle = \frac{1}{\sqrt{2}}(|1,0\rangle + |0,0\rangle)$$

$$|-,+\rangle = \frac{1}{\sqrt{2}}(|1,0\rangle - |0,0\rangle)$$

Substituting in, we obtain:

$$|\psi(t)\rangle = \cos\left(\frac{(\varepsilon_1-\varepsilon_2)t}{\hbar}\right)|1,0\rangle - i\sin\left(\frac{(\varepsilon_1-\varepsilon_2)t}{\hbar}\right)|0,0\rangle$$

The probability of observing $S = 1$ is

$$P_1 = \left|\sum_m \langle 1,m|\psi(t)\rangle\right|^2 = \cos^2\left(\frac{(\varepsilon_1-\varepsilon_2)t}{\hbar}\right)$$

and the probability of observing $S = 0$ is

$$P_0 = |\langle 0,0|\psi(t)\rangle|^2 = \sin^2\left(\frac{(\varepsilon_1-\varepsilon_2)t}{\hbar}\right)$$

Moreover, the expectation value of S^2 is

$$\langle \psi(t) | S^2 | \psi(t) \rangle = 2\hbar^2 \cos^2\left(\frac{(\varepsilon_1 - \varepsilon_2)t}{\hbar}\right)$$

(b) We consider an arbitrary initial state of the form

$$|\psi(0)\rangle = \alpha|+,+\rangle + \beta|+,-\rangle + \gamma|-,+\rangle + \delta|-,-\rangle$$

where $\alpha, \beta, \gamma, \delta$ are complex constants. In this case, the evolution of $|\psi(t)\rangle$ is given by

$$|\psi(t)\rangle = \alpha\tau_{++}|+,+\rangle + \beta\tau_{+-}|+,-\rangle + \gamma\tau_{-+}|-,+\rangle + \delta\tau_{--}|-,-\rangle$$

where $\tau_{\pm\pm} = \exp[(\mp\varepsilon_1 \mp \varepsilon_2)t/\hbar]$. Now we can calculate the expectation value of S^2:

$$\langle S^2 \rangle = 2\hbar^2 \left\{ |\alpha|^2 + |\delta|^2 + \frac{1}{2}\left(|\beta|^2 + |\gamma|^2\right) + \mathrm{Re}\left[\beta^* \gamma e^{2i(\varepsilon_1 - \varepsilon_2)t/\hbar}\right] \right\}$$

Clearly this expectation value is characterized by only one Bohr frequency:

$$\omega_B = \frac{2(\varepsilon_1 - \varepsilon_2)}{\hbar}$$

Solved Problem 14.4 A hydrogen-like atom is placed in a weak magnetic field $\vec{B} = B\hat{z}$, where the interaction is described by the *Zeeman hamiltonian*, $H' = \mu_B B(L_z + 2S_z)/\hbar$.

(a) Assume that in the absence of the $\vec{B}$ wave functions of the atom are eigenfunctions of L^2, S^2, J^2, J_z where $\vec{J} = \vec{L} + \vec{S}$. Use first-order perturbation theory to calculate the energy splittings caused by the magnetic field.

(b) The electron of such an atom is excited into a p-state. Into how many components does each of the levels split when a weak magnetic field is applied?

Solution.

(a) The perturbing Zeeman hamiltonian can be written as

$$H' = \frac{\mu_B B \left(J_z + S_z \right)}{\hbar}$$

where μ_B is the Bohr magneton. The energy levels, $E = E(n,\ell,J) + \Delta E$ of the complete hamiltonian, $H = H_0 + H_{so} + H'$ are then given by the previously-known energies plus the perturbation

$$\Delta E = \mu_B B \left\langle \ell \pm \frac{1}{2}, M \left| \left(J_z + S_z \right) \right| \ell \pm \frac{1}{2}, M \right\rangle$$

$$\Delta E = \mu_B B \left[1 \pm \frac{1}{2\ell + 1} \right]$$

(b) In the absence of a magnetic field, there are two degenerate energy levels, which are specified by the quantum numbers ($\ell = 1, J = 1/2$). When the magnetic field is applied, the degeneracy is removed. The $J = \dfrac{3}{2}$ level is split into four components since $M = \dfrac{-3}{2}, \dfrac{-1}{2}, \dfrac{1}{2}, \dfrac{3}{2}$. Similarly, the $J = \dfrac{1}{2}$ level is split into two components corresponding to $M = \dfrac{-1}{2}, \dfrac{1}{2}$.

The energy changes are given by the equation above. Thus

$$\Delta E(\ell,J) = g(\ell,J)\mu_B BM$$

where the *Lande factor* is

$$g(\ell,J) = 1 \pm \frac{1}{2\ell + 1}$$

Chapter 15
SCATTERING
THEORY

IN THIS CHAPTER:

- ✔ *Cross Section*
- ✔ *Stationary Scattering States*
- ✔ *Born Approximation*
- ✔ *Partial Wave Expansions*
- ✔ *Scattering of Identical Particles*

Cross Section

Consider a typical scattering problem. A beam of particles scatters from the potential $V(\vec{r})$ with coordinate origin at point O. We define the *differential cross section*, $d\sigma/d\Omega$, as the ratio of the number of scattered particles $dn(\theta,\varphi)$ per unit time within the *solid angle* $d\Omega$ divided by the incident particle *flux*, F

$$\frac{d\sigma}{d\Omega} = \frac{dn(\theta,\varphi)}{Fd\Omega}$$

where $d\sigma/d\Omega$ has the dimension of a surface.

Note!

We assume any interaction between the scattered particles is negligible, multiple scattering processes are negligible, and the incident beam width is much larger than a typical range for the scattering potential (so that the particle has well-defined momentum).

The *total cross section* is obtained by integrating over $d\Omega$:

$$\sigma_T = \int \frac{d\sigma}{d\Omega} d\Omega$$

When the scattering is from a potential $V(\vec{r})$, the differential cross section is the same in the lab and center of mass (CM) frames:

$$\left(\frac{d\sigma}{d\Omega} \right)^{Lab} = \left(\frac{d\sigma}{d\Omega} \right)^{CM}$$

However, if we consider electric scattering of particle 1 from particle 2, then the differential cross section in the two frames will be different, and is given by

$$\left(\frac{d\sigma}{d\Omega} \right)^{Lab} = \frac{\left(1 + \gamma^2 + 2\gamma \cos\theta \right)^{3/2}}{\left| 1 + \gamma \cos\theta \right|} \left(\frac{d\sigma}{d\Omega} \right)^{CM}$$

where θ is the scattering angle in the CM frame and $\gamma = \dfrac{m_1}{m_2}$.

Stationary Scattering States

Consider a scattering problem relating to particles with mass μ and well-defined momentum $\vec{p} = \hbar \vec{k}$, which scatter from a time-independent potential $V(\vec{r})$. The hamiltonian of the system is

$$H = H_0 + V(\vec{r})$$

where H_0 is the free hamiltonian. The wave function for a scattered particle with energy $E > 0$ is obtained by solving the stationary Schrödinger equation:

$$[\nabla^2 + k^2 - U(\vec{r})]\varphi(\vec{r}) = 0$$

where

$$k = \sqrt{\frac{2\mu E}{\hbar^2}}$$

$$U(\vec{r}) = \frac{2\mu}{\hbar^2} V(\vec{r})$$

For a collision between two particles, $V(\vec{r})$ is the interaction potential between them and E is the kinetic energy associated with the particle of reduced mass μ in the CM frame.

For a potential $V(\vec{r})$ of shorter range than the Coulomb potential, the solution of the Schrödinger equation can be written as a composition of an incident plane wave and a spherical wave of amplitude $f(\theta,\varphi)$:

$$\varphi(r)\big|_{r \to \infty} \to e^{ikz} + f(\theta,\varphi)\frac{e^{ikr}}{r}$$

The *scattering amplitude* is given by

$$f_k(\theta,\varphi) = \frac{-1}{4\pi} \int e^{-i\vec{k}_f \cdot \vec{r}'} U(\vec{r}')\varphi(\vec{r}')d^3r'$$

where $k_f = \dfrac{\vec{k} \cdot \vec{r}}{r}$. The amplitude $f_k(\theta,\varphi)$ depends on the potential and the scattering angles. This quantity is directly related to the differential cross section:

$$\frac{d\sigma(\theta,\varphi)}{d\Omega} = \left| f_k(\theta,\varphi) \right|^2$$

Born Approximation

The Born approximation is obtained by treating the potential $U(\vec{r})$ as a small perturbation.

Remember

The Born approximation of the scattering amplitude is

$$f_k^B(\theta,\varphi) = \frac{-1}{4\pi}\int e^{-i\vec{q}\cdot\vec{r}'} U(\vec{r}')\varphi(\vec{r}')d^3r'$$

where $\vec{q} = \vec{k}_f - \vec{k}_i$ is the difference of the final and initial momenta, the *momentum transfer*. Note that in the Born approximation the scattering amplitude is proportional to the Fourier transform of the potential with respect to $\vec{q}$.

If the potential has spherical symmetry, $U(\vec{r}) = U(r)$, and we can simplify by taking $\vec{q}$ as the polar axis and integrating over $d\Omega'$:

$$f_k^B(\theta,\varphi) = \frac{-2\mu}{\hbar^2 q}\int_{-\infty}^{\infty} \sin(qr)\, rV(r)\, dr$$

where

$$q = 2k\sin\left(\frac{\theta}{2}\right)$$

is the *momentum transfer* and $k = |\vec{k}_f| = |\vec{k}_i|$. The Born approximation is valid when either of the following conditions holds:

$$\bar{V} \ll \frac{\hbar^2}{\mu a^2} \quad \text{where} \quad ka \leq 1$$

$$\bar{V} \ll \left(\frac{\hbar^2}{\mu a^2}\right) ka \quad \text{where} \quad ka \gg 1$$

where a is the range of the potential and $\bar{V}$ is the "averaged" potential defined by

$$\bar{V} = \frac{1}{4\pi a^2} \int \frac{V(r)}{r} d^3 r$$

The second condition shows that the Born approximation is always applicable for sufficiently fast (high energy) particles. This condition is weaker than the first one; hence, if the potential can be regarded as a perturbation at low energies, it can always be so regarded at high energies, whereas the converse is not necessarily true.

Solved Problem 15.1 A particle of mass μ and momentum $\vec{p} = \hbar\vec{k}$ is scattered by the potential $V(\vec{r}) = \frac{e^{-r/a}}{r} V_0 a,$ where V_0 and $a > 0$ are real constants (Yukawa potential).

(a) Using the Born approximation, calculate the differential cross section.

(b) Obtain the total cross section.

Solution.

(a) The range of the Yukawa potential is characterized by the distance a. We assume that $V_0 a^2 \ll \frac{\hbar^2}{\mu}$ so that the Born approximation is valid for all the values of ka. The scattering amplitude is then given by

$$f(\theta, \varphi) = \frac{-1}{4\pi} \frac{2\mu V_0 a}{\hbar^2} \int e^{-i\vec{q}\cdot\vec{r}} \frac{e^{-r/r_0}}{r} d^3 r$$

Since the potential has spherical symmetry, we can carry out the integration using the relation

$$\int r^2 e^{-i\vec{q}\cdot\vec{r}} V(r) dr d\Omega = \frac{4\pi}{q} \int \sin(qr) V(r) r dr$$

where $d\Omega = \sin\theta d\theta d\varphi$. Therefore,

$$f(\theta,\varphi) = \frac{-2\mu V_0 a^3}{\hbar^2 \left\{ 1 + \left[2ka\sin\frac{\theta}{2} \right]^2 \right\}}$$

Then we can write the differential cross section

$$\frac{d\sigma(\theta)}{d\Omega} = \frac{4\mu^2 V_0^2 a^6}{\hbar^4 \left\{ 1 + 4k^2 a^2 \sin^2\frac{\theta}{2} \right\}^2}$$

Note that because of the spherical symmetry, the differential cross section does not depend on the azimuthal angle.

(b) The total scattering cross section is obtained by integration

$$\sigma = \frac{4\mu^2 V_0^2 a^6 (4\pi)}{\hbar^4 \left\{ 1 + 4k^2 a^2 \right\}}$$

Note that in the infinite range limit ($a \rightarrow \infty$, $V_0 \rightarrow 0$, and $V_0 a \rightarrow Z_1 Z_2 e^2$), the Yukawa potential corresponds to the Coulomb interaction between two ions. Notice that in the same limit, the result of (a) reduces to the familiar *Rutherford formula*.

Solved Problem 15.2 Show that if the scattering potential has a translation invariance property, $V(\vec{r} + \vec{R}) = V(\vec{r})$, where $\vec{R}$ is a constant vector, then the Born approximation scattering vanishes unless $\vec{q} \cdot \vec{R} = 2\pi n$, where n is an integer.

Solution. The translation symmetry of the potential implies

$$\int e^{-i\vec{q}\cdot\vec{r}} V(\vec{r}) d^3r = \int e^{-i\vec{q}\cdot\vec{r}} V(\vec{r} + \vec{R}) d^3r$$

By changing variables, $\vec{r} \rightarrow \vec{r} + \vec{R}$, on the right-hand side, we obtain

$$\int e^{-i\vec{q}\cdot\vec{r}}V(\vec{r})d^3r = \int e^{-i\vec{q}\cdot\vec{r}}e^{i\vec{q}\cdot\vec{R}}V(\vec{r}\,')d^3r'$$

Therefore,

$$\int e^{-i\vec{q}\cdot\vec{R}}V(\vec{r})\left[1 - e^{i\vec{q}\cdot\vec{R}}\right]d^3r = 0$$

This is true when either of the following two conditions is satisfied:

$$\int e^{-i\vec{q}\cdot\vec{r}}V(\vec{r})d^3r = 0$$

$$\vec{q}\cdot\vec{R} = 2\pi n$$

The Born scattering amplitude is proportional to the Fourier transform of the potential. We therefore conclude that it vanishes identically unless the second of these conditions is met. Normally,

$$f^B(\vec{q}) = \sum_{\vec{k}} f_{\vec{q}}\delta_{\vec{q}\vec{k}}$$

Note that the translation symmetry of the scattering potential corresponds to the scattering form of a lattice. For any vector $\vec{R}$ of the lattice, the set of vectors $\vec{k}$ that satisfy $\vec{k}\cdot\vec{R} = 2\pi n$ constitutes the reciprocal lattice. Therefore, the scattering amplitude vanishes unless the momentum transfer $\vec{q}$ is equal to some vector of the reciprocal lattice. This is precisely the *Bragg-Von Laue scattering condition*.

Partial Wave Expansions

Consider a potential with spherical symmetry, $V(\vec{r}) = V(r)$. In this case, the stationary wave function $\varphi_k(r,\theta)$ and the scattering amplitude $f_k(\theta)$ can be expanded in terms of Legendre polynomials:

$$\varphi_k(r,\theta) = \sum_{\ell=0}^{\infty} A_\ell \frac{\chi_\ell(r)P_\ell(\cos\theta)}{r}$$

$$f_k(\theta) = \sum_{\ell=0}^{\infty}(2\ell+1)f_\ell P_\ell(\cos\theta)$$

where the coefficients A_ℓ, f_ℓ and the functions $\chi_\ell(r)$ are to be determined. The radial Schrödinger equation gives

$$\left[\frac{d^2}{dr^2} + k^2 - U(r) - \frac{\ell(\ell+1)}{r^2}\right]\chi_\ell(r) = 0$$

where the boundary condition is $\chi_\ell(0) = 0$. In the asymptotic region

$$\lim_{r \to \infty} \chi_\ell(r) \to \frac{1}{k}C_\ell \sin\left(kr - \frac{\pi\ell}{2} + \delta_\ell\right)$$

The parameter δ_ℓ is called the *phase shift*, since it determines the difference in phase between this solution and that of the free radial Schrödinger equation.

Similarly, we can expand plane waves in terms of the Legendre polynomials

$$e^{ikz} = e^{ikr\cos\theta} = \sum_{\ell=0}^{\infty} i^\ell (2\ell+1)\left(e^{2i\delta_\ell} - 1\right)P_\ell(\cos\theta)$$

Now substituting these expansions, we obtain

$$A_\ell = (2\ell+1)i^\ell e^{i\delta_\ell}$$

$$f_k(\theta) = \frac{1}{2ik}\sum_{\ell=0}^{\infty}(2\ell+1)\left(e^{2i\delta_\ell} - 1\right)P_\ell(\cos\theta)$$

Thus, the differential cross section is given by

$$\frac{d\sigma}{d\Omega} = \frac{1}{k^2}\left|\sum_{\ell=0}^{\infty}(2\ell+1)e^{i\delta_\ell}\sin\delta_\ell P_\ell(\cos\theta)\right|^2$$

and the total cross section is

$$\sigma_T = \frac{4\pi}{k^2}\sum_{\ell=0}^{\infty}(2\ell+1)\sin^2\delta_\ell$$

From these we could verify the *optical theorem*:

$$\sigma_T = \frac{4\pi}{k}\,\text{Im}\left(f_k(0)\right)$$

The phase shifts, δ_ℓ, are completely determined by the asymptotic form of the radial function. The partial wave expansion is particularly useful for short-range potentials that vanish outside the region $r < a$ since in that case the partial waves that satisfy $\ell(\ell+1) > ka$ may be neglected. Moreover, since the radial wave function and its derivative are continuous at the boundary $r = a$, we have

$$\tan \delta_\ell = \frac{k j_\ell'(ka) - \gamma_\ell j_\ell(ka)}{k n_\ell'(ka) - \gamma_\ell n_\ell(ka)}$$

where the j_ℓ and n_ℓ are the spherical Bessel and Neumann functions, respectively, and γ_ℓ is the logarithmic derivative, defined as

$$\gamma_\ell = \frac{1}{R_\ell} \frac{dR_\ell}{dr}\bigg|_{r=a^-} \quad where \quad R_\ell = \frac{\chi_\ell}{r}$$

For sufficiently weak potential for which the Born approximation holds, all the phase shifts are small and are given by

$$\sin \delta_\ell \approx \delta_\ell = \frac{-2\mu}{\hbar^2} \int V(r) j_\ell^2(kr) dr$$

Solved Problem 15.3 A particle of mass μ is scattered from a spherical repelling potential of radius R:

$$V(r) = \begin{cases} V_0 & for \quad r \le R \\ 0 & for \quad r > R \end{cases}$$

(a) Using the Born approximation, calculate the total cross section in the limit of low energy.

(b) Repeat the calculation of total cross section using the partial wave expansion, and considering only the s-wave contribution.

Solution.

(a) The scattering amplitude in the Born approximation is

$$f_k^B(\theta) = \frac{-2\mu V_0 4\pi}{4\pi\hbar^2 q}\int_0^\infty \sin(qr)\,r\,dr = \frac{-2\mu V_0}{\hbar^2 q}\left[\frac{\sin(qR)}{q^2} - \frac{R\cos(qR)}{q}\right]$$

In the limit $qR \to 0$ this leads to the isotropic cross section

$$\frac{d\sigma^B}{d\Omega} = \frac{4\mu^2 V_0^2 R^6}{9\hbar^4}$$

so that the total cross section is given by

$$\sigma_T^B = \frac{16\pi\mu^2 V_0^2 R^6}{9\hbar^4}$$

(b) In the limit $E \to 0$ it is sufficient to consider only s-wave scattering. In order to determine the phase shift δ_0 we examine the radial Schrödinger equation for $\chi_0(r)$:

$$\left[\frac{d^2}{dr^2} + \frac{2\mu E}{\hbar^2}\right]\chi_0^1(r) = 0 \quad \text{for} \quad r > R$$

$$\left[\frac{d^2}{dr^2} + \frac{2\mu}{\hbar^2}(E - V_0)\right]\chi_0^2(r) = 0 \quad \text{for} \quad r \le R$$

to determine the solutions

$$\chi_0^1(r) = A\sin(kr + \delta_0)$$

$$\chi_0^2(r) = B\sinh\left(kr\sqrt{\frac{V_0}{E} - 1}\right)$$

where $k = \sqrt{\dfrac{2\mu E}{\hbar^2}}$ and $V_0 \gg E$. These solutions satisfy the boundary conditions

$$\chi_0^1(R) = \chi_0^2(R)$$

$$\chi_0^{\prime(1)}(R) = \chi_0^{\prime(2)}(R)$$

These give

$$\delta_0 = \sqrt{\frac{E}{V_0}} \tanh\left(KR\right) - kR$$

$$f_0\left(\theta\right) = \frac{1}{k} e^{i\delta_0} \sin \delta_0$$

where $K = k\sqrt{\frac{V_0}{E} - 1}$. Finally, the total cross section is

$$\sigma_T^0 \approx 4\pi R^2 \left[1 - \frac{\tanh\left(KR\right)}{KR}\right]^2$$

Note that the answers to (a) and (b) coincide only in the limit of a very short-range potential. Note also that although both methods lead to isotropic differential cross section, the Born approximation involves a violation of the optical theorem.

Scattering of Identical Particles

The case where two identical particles collide requires special consideration. If the total spin of the system is even (+) or odd (−), the differential cross section is

$$\frac{d\sigma}{d\Omega} = \left|f\left(\theta\right) \pm f\left(\pi - \theta\right)\right|^2$$

For example, if $s = 1/2$, the spin wave function can be in singlet (total spin is 0) or triplet (total spin is 1) states.

For an unpolarized beam of particles with spin s, the system can be in $(2s + 1)^2$ spin states that are distributed with equal probability. From the total number of possibilities, $(2s + 1)$ spin states are antisymmetric. Therefore, the differential cross section is

$$\frac{d\sigma}{d\Omega} = \left|f\left(\theta\right)\right|^2 + \left|f\left(\pi - \theta\right)\right|^2 + \frac{(-1)^{2s}}{2s + 1} 2\,\mathrm{Re}\left[f\left(\theta\right) f^*\left(\pi - \theta\right)\right]$$

Chapter 16

THE SEMICLASSICAL TREATMENT OF RADIATION

Interaction of Radiation with Atomic Systems

The hamiltonian of a particle with mass m, charge e, and spin $\vec{S}$ in an external electromagnetic field is given by

$$H = \frac{1}{2m}\left(\vec{p} - \frac{e}{c}\vec{A}\right)^2 + V(\vec{r}) + e\varphi - \frac{e}{mc}\vec{S}\cdot\vec{B}$$

where $\vec{A}$ is the vector potential, φ is the scalar potential, and $\vec{B} = \vec{\nabla} \times \vec{A}$ is the magnetic field. It is possible to choose a gauge for which H will be simpler.

You Need to Know ✔

The gauge generally employed in problems dealing with radiation is the *Coulomb gauge*, which is also called the *radiation gauge* or the *transverse gauge*, where we choose

$$\vec{\nabla} \times \vec{A} = 0$$
$$\varphi = 0$$

Thus, the hamiltonian becomes

$$H = \left[\frac{p^2}{2m} + V(\vec{r}) \right] + \left[\frac{e^2}{2mc^2} A^2 - \frac{e}{mc} \left(\vec{A} \cdot \vec{p} + \vec{S} \cdot \vec{B} \right) \right]$$

where we recognize the familiar, unperturbed hamiltonian, H_0, and the new term, which we will call H'. For a semiclassical treatment of radiation, we assume that the term A^2 is very small and negligible. In this case,

$$H' = \frac{-e}{mc} \left(\vec{A} \cdot \vec{p} + \vec{S} \cdot \vec{B} \right)$$

This limit is called the *low-intensity limit*.

Time-Dependent Perturbation Theory

In the low-intensity limit, $H'(t)$ can be treated as a small time-dependent perturbation. If the system is initially in the state $|i\rangle$ and the perturbation is turned on at $t = 0$, the first-order amplitude for finding the system in the state $|f\rangle$ at time t is given by

$$a_{fi}^{(1)}(t) = \frac{1}{i\hbar} \int_0^t e^{i\omega_{fi}t'} \langle f|H'(t')|i\rangle \, dt'$$

where $\hbar\omega_{fi} = E_f - E_i$. In a semiclassical treatment, we usually assume that the electromagnetic field $\vec{A}$ is described by a plane wave:

$$\vec{A}(\vec{r},t) = 2|A_0|\hat{e}\cos(\vec{k}\cdot\vec{r} - \omega t + \theta)$$

where $A_0 = |A_0|e^{i\theta}$ is a complex number, $\hat{e}$ is a unit vector in the direction of polarization, $\vec{k}$ is the wave vector, and $\hat{\varepsilon}\cdot\vec{k} = 0$ (transverse gauge). Therefore,

$$a_{fi}^{(1)}(t) = -\left(\frac{e^{i(\omega_{fi}-\omega)t}-1}{\omega_{fi}-\omega}\right)\frac{T_{fi}^+}{\hbar} - \left(\frac{e^{i(\omega_{fi}+\omega)t}-1}{\omega_{fi}+\omega}\right)\frac{T_{fi}^-}{\hbar}$$

where

$$T_{fi}^{\pm} = \frac{-e}{mc}\langle f|e^{\pm i\vec{k}\cdot\vec{r}}A_0^*\left[\hat{\varepsilon}\cdot\vec{p}\pm i\vec{S}\cdot\left(\vec{k}\times\hat{\varepsilon}\right)\right]|i\rangle$$

Transition Rate

Consider the transition amplitude $a_{fi}^{(1)}(t)$. A resonant transition is obtained when the frequency of the external radiation field is close to one of the characteristic frequencies of the unperturbed system, i.e. $\omega \approx \pm\omega_{fi}$. In this case, one can neglect the interference term and distinguish between *resonant absorption* ($\omega_{fi} > 0$) and *resonant emission* ($\omega_{fi} < 0$). The transition probability is then given by

$$P_{fi} \cong \frac{|T_{fi}^+|}{\hbar^2}\left\{\frac{\sin\left[\left(\omega_{fi}-\omega\right)t/2\right]}{\left(\omega_{fi}-\omega\right)/2}\right\}^2$$

for resonant absorption and

$$P_{fi} \cong \frac{|T_{fi}^-|}{\hbar^2}\left\{\frac{\sin\left[\left(\omega_{fi}+\omega\right)t/2\right]}{\left(\omega_{fi}+\omega\right)/2}\right\}^2$$

for induced emission. For a strictly monochromatic field, these transition probabilities depend strongly on the difference $\omega - |\omega_{fi}|$, and lead to a non-stationary transition rate. A transition probability that is linear in time (a constant transition rate) is obtained if one considers the transition from an initial state $|i\rangle$ to a continuum of final states $|f\rangle$. In this case the transition rate is obtained by using Fermi's golden rule:

$$W_{fi}^{\pm} = \frac{dP^{\pm}(t)}{dt} = \frac{2\pi}{\hbar}\left|\langle f|T^{\pm}|i\rangle\right|^{2} \rho\left(E_{f} = E_{i} \pm \hbar\omega\right)$$

where $\rho(E_f)$ is the density of final states. Similarly, when the radiation field is not monochromatic, but rather contains a spectrum of frequencies $u(\omega)$, the transition rate is

$$W_{fi} = \frac{4\pi^{2}e^{2}u\left(\omega_{fi}\right)}{m^{2}\hbar^{2}\omega_{fi}^{2}}\left|\langle f|e^{\pm i\vec{k}\cdot\vec{r}}\left[\hat{\varepsilon}\cdot\vec{p} \pm i\vec{S}\cdot\left(\vec{k}\times\hat{\varepsilon}\right)\right]|i\rangle\right|^{2}$$

where $|i\rangle$ and $|f\rangle$ are the initial and final (discrete) states, and the plus and minus signs correspond to absorption and emission, respectively.

Multipole Transitions

In the long wavelength approximation,

$$e^{\pm i\vec{k}\cdot\vec{r}} \approx 1 + i\vec{k}\cdot\vec{r} + \cdots$$

we can write $T_{fi}^{\pm}$ using a multipole expansion:

$$T_{fi}^{\pm} \approx \langle f|\left\{im\omega_{fi}\hat{\varepsilon}\cdot\vec{r} + \frac{i}{2}\left(\vec{L}+2\vec{S}\right)\cdot\left(\vec{k}\times\hat{\varepsilon}\right) - \frac{m\omega_{fi}}{2}\left(\vec{k}\cdot\vec{r}\right)\hat{\varepsilon}\cdot\vec{r}\right\}|i\rangle$$

The first term corresponds to an *electric dipole transition*, the second to a *magnetic dipole transition*, and the third term to an *electric quadrupole transition*. Usually the transition rate is dominated by the electric dipole term; in this case the transition rate is

$$W_{fi} = \frac{4\pi^{2}e^{2}u\left(\omega_{fi}\right)}{\hbar^{2}}\left|\langle f|\hat{\varepsilon}\cdot\vec{r}|i\rangle\right|^{2}$$

However, for some particular states $|i\rangle$ and $|f\rangle$, this matrix element may vanish, in which case this transition is called *forbidden*. Note that for an isotropic external radiation field, the polarization vector $\hat{e}$ is randomly oriented. Averaging the components of the unit vector $\hat{e}$ over all angles gives

$$W_{fi} = \frac{4\pi^2 e^2 u\left(\omega_{fi}\right)}{3\hbar^2}\left|\langle f|\vec{r}|i\rangle\right|^2 \equiv B_{fi}u\left(\omega_{fi}\right)$$

B_{fi} are known as the *Einstein coefficients* for absorption and induced emission.

Solved Problem 16.1 Find the selection rules for emission and absorption of:

(a) electric dipole radiation

(b) magnetic dipole radiation, by an electron in an central potential.

Solution.

(a) To obtain the selection rules for electric dipole transitions, we consider matrix elements of the form $\langle f|r_k|i\rangle$ where $|i\rangle$ and $|f\rangle$ are the initial and final eigenstates of an electron moving in a central potential and $k = x,y,z$. The unperturbed wave function is then

$$\psi_{n_i\ell_i m_i} = R_{n_i\ell_i}Y_{\ell_i}^{m_i}(\theta,\varphi)$$
$$\psi_{n_f\ell_f m_f} = R_{n_f\ell_f}Y_{\ell_f}^{m_f}(\theta,\varphi)$$

In the representation of spherical harmonics,

$$x \pm iy = \mp\sqrt{\frac{8\pi}{3}}rY_1^{\pm1}(\theta,\varphi)$$

$$z = \sqrt{\frac{4\pi}{3}}rY_1^0(\theta,\varphi)$$

Therefore, the matrix elements are proportional to the corresponding angular integrals, for example,

$$\langle f|z|i\rangle \propto \int \left(Y_{\ell_f}^{m_f}\right)^* Y_1^0 Y_{\ell_i}^{m_i}\, d\Omega$$

This is different from zero only if $\Delta\ell = \pm 1$ and $\Delta m = 0$. When we collect the similar results for the other matrix elements, we find that for electric dipole transitions:

$$\Delta\ell = \pm 1$$
$$\Delta m = 0, \pm 1$$

(b) The selection rules for magnetic dipole transitions are found from matrix elements of the form $\langle f|L_k|i\rangle$. From the general properties of angular momentum, we immediately find

$$\langle f|L_z|i\rangle \propto \hbar m_i \delta_{\ell_f \ell_i} \delta_{m_f m_i}$$

When we collect the similar results for the other matrix elements, we find that for magnetic dipole transitions:

$$\Delta\ell = 0$$
$$\Delta m = 0, \pm 1$$

Spontaneous Emission

An excited atomic system can also emit radiation in the absence of an external radiation field. The transition rate for spontaneous transition, in the dipole approximation, is given by

$$W_{fi} = \frac{4e^2 \omega_{fi}^3}{3\hbar c^3} \left|\langle f|\vec{r}|i\rangle\right|^2 \equiv A_{fi}$$

where A_{fi} is the Einstein coefficient for spontaneous emission.

Solved Problem 16.2 Find the probability per unit time of spontaneous transition for a hydrogen atom in the first excited state.

Solution. The probability per unit time for the transition $2p \to 1s$ (emission) is given by

$$W_{1s2p} = u(\omega_{21})B_{1s2p} + A_{1s2p}$$

Thus we obtain

$$W_{1s2p} = \frac{4\pi^2 e^2}{3\hbar^2}\left[u(\omega_{21}) + \frac{\hbar\omega_{21}^3}{\pi^2 c^3} \right]\left| \langle 100|\vec{r}|21m'\rangle \right|^2$$

In particular, for a hydrogen atom in the first excited state,

$$\left| \langle 100|\vec{r}|21m'\rangle \right|^2 = \frac{5}{9}a_0^2$$

Therefore,

$$A_{1s2p} = \frac{20}{27}\frac{e^2 \omega_{21}^3}{\hbar c^3}a_0^2 = \frac{20}{27}\frac{\omega_{21}^3}{c^4}\frac{\hbar^2}{m^2 \alpha}$$

where α is the *fine structure constant*. However,

$$\hbar\omega_{21} = \frac{3}{4}\frac{\alpha^2 mc^2}{2}$$

Hence,

$$A_{1s2p} = \frac{5}{48}\alpha^3 \omega_{21} \approx 6 \times 10^{-8}\ \text{sec}^{-1}$$

This leads to a radiative lifetime on the order of 1.5×10^{-9} sec.

Index